WEBSTER BOOTH & ANNE ZIEGLER:
EXCERPTS FROM
GRAMOPHONE & DISCOGRAPHY

Compiled by

JEAN COLLEN

Webster Booth & Anne Ziegler

INTRODUCTION

The first part of this book is a compilation of reviews and articles from *The Gramophone* online archive, referring to Webster Booth and/or Anne Ziegler.

The second part contains my own compilation of a discography of solo and duet recordings of Anne Ziegler and Webster Booth, including recordings made with other singers, the HMV Light Opera Company and recordings marked only with "with vocal refrain". Most of the recordings in the discography are solo recordings by Webster Booth. I have marked duet recordings with Anne Ziegler, Anne Ziegler's solos, and recordings which do not acknowledge Webster Booth (such as the HMV Light Opera Company and those marked "with vocal refrain") with the following markers:

*Duets
#Anne Ziegler solos
+With vocal refrain

I have also included a list of some of their many broadcasts, but only those where recordings exist - either in the National Sound Archive - or in my own collection.

The film, musical, opera and oratorio from which a particular song or aria comes is marked in bold. The name of the accompanist, orchestra, and conductor (if known) follows. I have included the place where the recording took place (if known) and dates of the recordings (if known).

This discography is as complete as I could make it, but it is possible that some recordings are missing. I was unable to trace all the record numbers in the HMV B series and have listed these at the end of the HMV list. I welcome any further information so that I can update the list. The 78 rpm records are listed first, followed by compilations on long playing records, compact discs and broadcasts.

CONTENTS

GRAMOPHONE EXCERPTS

1/1 – NINETEEN-THIRTIES

5. I Love the Moon—A brown bird singing. Webster Booth
B3319, 3/-

May 1930
Webster Booth (tenor) B3319 (10", 3/-) – An emotional, but restrained record of Wood's (Haydn – certainly not Charles or Henry) *A Brown Bird Singing* and Rubens's *I Love the Moon*, accompanied by a small orchestra and an orchestral canary in full song. There are one or two of the vulgar abuses of which we are so very sick – e.g. the plunge into a foreign key, a very telling device which had, originally, its legitimate, but highly special, use. CM Crabtree.

April 1931
Webster Booth has two good waltz songs from the film **One Heavenly Night** (HMV B3778, 3/-) which could hardly be better treated.

May 1931

The New Mayfair Orchestra is reduced to playing *Somewhere a Voice is Calling* and *I Know of Two Bright Eyes* (HMV B3735, 3/-). These would be succulent enough if the singer Webster Booth had not had the key awkwardly changed in the former, a small point which might spoil the suavity of the performance for the listener.

September 1931

Abridged Gilbert and Sullivan

Dr Malcolm Sargent has conducted an abridged version of Gilbert and Sullivan's **The Gondoliers** with a delicacy and suavity that will commend the work of the chorus and soloists to a multitude of those who had to deny themselves the complete album. In its present form the six 10in records (HMVB3866-71) in album with book of the words contain the quintessence of the opera: the characters are very clearly differentiated by the soloists. Sydney Granville as the Grand Inquisitor is perhaps not entirely satisfactory, and Beatrice Elwen sings *When a Merry Maiden Marries* without making all the points; but the splendid support of Derek Oldham, George Baker, Webster Booth and Essie Ackland ensures a polish and sense of the words that it would be hard to match. B3869 containing the quartet *Then One of Us will be a Queen*, Marcus and Giuseppe's duet and Finale of Act 1, and B3870, Leslie Rands in *Rising Early in the Morning* and Derek Oldham in *Take a Pair of Sparkling Eyes* would be my choice of samples. The supervision of the production by Rupert D'Oyly Carte gives the stamp of authority, if such were needed, to the work of abridgement.

February 1932

The music from **Rose Marie** is ever popular and a Decca **Selection of Vocal Gems** is excellently sung by Anne Welch, Webster Booth and Victor Conway (Decca K628, 12", 2/6d)

April 1932

There are not many selections this month. **Goodnight Vienna** is on its way and will probably be on view to London film-goers by the time you get your April *Gramophone*, so that you will like to know how the music sounds, and will welcome a **Vocal Selection** by Olive Groves and Webster Booth on Decca K644 (12", 2/6d)

May 1932

Olive Groves and Webster Booth are particularly good in a *Vocal Selection* from **Goodnight Vienna** (Decca K644, 2/6d)

April 1933

Webster Booth vo.   London, c 1 feb. 1933

E-1171-A **WHAT MORE CAN I ASK?** * / **BRIGHTER THAN**
           THE SUN **- FROM THE BRITISH & DOMINION FILM
           "THE LITTLE DAMOZEL" - AW vo * SB vo **   SUPER durium M-1
E-1172-A-B **TELL ME TO-NIGHT** VOCAL FOXTROT MISCHA
           SPOLIANSKY FRANK EYTON - WB vo   SUPER durium M-4
           PARLEZ-MOI D'AMOUR WALTZ SONG JEAN LENOIR
           BRUCE SIEVIER - WB vo   SUPER durium M-4

March 1934
Regal-Zonophone (1/6)
Then, if you like old favourites, Fred Hartley's Quintet, with Webster Booth singing, in **Bird Songs at Eventide** and **Roses of Picardy** (MR1220).

June 1934
Webster Booth continues to be the principal attraction of Fred Hartley's records and his singing of **Toselli's Serenade** and **In Old Madrid** to the accompaniment of the Quintet is first-class (MR1288).

July 1935
The most important vocal record is the first of a new series from Columbia under the general heading of **West End Nights**. This (DX691) has tunes from **Glamorous Night**, **Gay Deceivers** and **Stop Press**. The singers are Muriel Barron, Marjorie Stedeford and Webster Booth with chorus and orchestra. A special welcome to Mr Booth, whose singing with Fred Hartley is such a delight – definitely our best light tenor. The performance is 100 per cent better than the material. However, it is something in these days to be able to make composers happy.

September 1935
As we go to press, comes a record by Webster Booth, on HMV B8360. Mr Booth, lately starring in **My Kingdom for a Cow**, makes a welcome appearance in Sanderson's ever-popular *As I Sit Here* and *Love Passes By*. I shall hope to hear him soon in worthier material. R W

November 1935
WEBSTER BOOTH by W S Meadmore.

Over six feet in height, dark and slim, Webster Booth is the Valentino of tenors. The combination of a pleasing stage appearance and a really good tenor voice is rare; among contemporary English singers I can think of only one other who, besides Booth, possesses both. Booth also has the unusual compass of two octaves and two notes. Herman Finck said of the top D flat which Booth used in **The Three Musketeers** that it was the highest tenor note he had ever heard sung in Drury Lane Theatre.

One of six children, Webster Booth early showed a predilection for music in a family that was almost entirely unmusical, although his mother, as a young girl, had played the organ in a chapel. Born in Birmingham, Booth was a chorister at Lincoln Cathedral for four and a half years. He was thirteen when his broke; he returned home, and for two years studied accountancy. Then he made a start in life in an accountant's office.

He met Richard Wassell, then conductor of the Birmingham orchestra. Wassell thought highly of the promise of his voice and gave him lessons at Bantock's school.

Professional engagements to sing at concerts soon followed; music began to clash with accountancy. Office hours were long and the bogey of further examinations demanded continuous evening study to ensure success. But booth's trial balances never agreed; his mind, which should have been intent on tracing errors, would be wondering whether he would be able to sing at a concert the following night, or whether he would have to cancel it at the last minute and go on an audit.

When the D'Oyly Carte Opera Company was giving a season in Birmingham, the conductor was so impressed that he wired to Rupert D'Oyly Carte, and Booth was asked to go to London for an interview. But the day fixed clashed with an audit which Booth had to do at Cardiff. To get to both places was impossible. Booth could not make up his mind what to do. If he went to London he would certainly lose his job, while if he kept his appointment at Cardiff a magnificent opportunity would be lost. Even on his way to the station he was in two minds. On one hand was comparative security, on the other the glorious uncertainty of the thing he really wanted to do. But Booth was young; the issue was never actually in doubt. At the booking office he burnt his boats and asked for a ticket to London.

The interview was highly satisfactory; he was given a contract to sing in the chorus. For four years he was with the D'Oyly Carte Company, becoming tenor understudy for thirteen operas and singing all the small tenor parts. The company went to Canada. On its return to England in 1927,

Webster Booth realised that it offered him little chance of further advancement, and he handed in his notice.

For the next few years he sang at London concerts in the winter, and like Leslie Henson, with seaside concert parties in the summer. For three summers he was with Powis Pinder, the old Savoyard, at Shanklin.

Webster Booth in 1935

His first stage engagement was in **The Three Musketeers** settled down for a long run. Unfortunately, long before, Booth had signed a contract to sing for the season at Blackpool. The Blackpool people refused, rather churlishly, to release him, and at the end of three months Booth had to leave the Lane and a reputation he was beginning to make. The bad luck of this setback was a great disappointment.

His association with the BBC dates from 1928. For two years he broadcast practically continuously, then, for no apparent reason, he was not given an engagement for four years! Suddenly rediscovered, he has broadcast for the last year in the oddest diversity of roles from singing with Fred Hartley's Novelty Quintet to playing the lead with Maria Elsner in **Countess Maritza**.

There was even an element of freakishness in his introduction to the gramophone. Invited to make a test record for Columbia, Joe Batten, the recording manager, was taken ill after the session, with the result that a verdict as to whether the record was issued or not was left in the air. But Webster Booth borrowed the record, and it was played over one night at a party. Peter Dawson happened to be present. He was enthusiastic, and asked Booth to meet him the next morning at the HMV recording studios.

Dawson took him into the studio and introduced him the manager with the words, "Have I ever brought you a dud?"

The record was played and made such an impression that Webster Booth was given a session there and then. The first record he made that morning was *Let Me Dream in Your Arms Again* (B3283).

Webster Booth's first film was in Buster Keaton's first talkie. Keaton did not have a word to say – Booth was the lead in the first English colour film, playing Faust to the Marguerite of Anne Ziegler. His last film experience has been in **The Robber Symphony**. Told that a large part of the film was to be shot in Dalmatia, Booth packed his trunks with summer clothes. On a Sunday evening he received a telephone message instructing him to leave for Badgastein the following morning. The voice advised him to take warm clothing. Where was Badgastein? Booth searched a map, and discovered that it was a town some 5000 feet high up in the Austrian Alps!

But there was no time left to make new purchases. On arrival Booth found that the temperature was 28 below zero, and that the work consisted of open-air shots in a forest, for which his costume was a dinner-suit! Every morning he rose at five. After having his hair curled by hand, the party hoisted themselves with the cameras on to wooden sleighs for an eight-mile journey up the mountains. When a virgin sheet of snow was found, Booth had to run across it in the direction of a poised camera. His run would start safely enough on surface snow barely covering the rock, but invariably a few paces would land him sprawling into a snowdrift. Twice his hands were frozen, but he says that it was a grand experience, and that he loved working with George Graves and Oscar Asche. The latter, whenever he was required to sit down, had to be supplied with two chairs!

Webster Booth married, in 1932, Paddy Prior, who had been playing leads in musical comedy long before they met. He was singing one night at the Concert Artistes Club (Association) and mechanically, as is his wont, fastened his eyes on someone in the audience. This person, to his surprise, seemed to be thoroughly enjoying his singing. The song was *One Alone* from **The Desert Song**, and the listener, to whom he was introduced later in the evening, was Paddy Prior.

Webster Booth prefers broadcasting and recording to any other type of work. He likes the atmosphere and good fellowship of studios, but does not feel so happy when facing an audience. He says that in a concert hall there is always a percentage of the audience who is bored with him, but, perforce, has to listen, while, if they listen-in to him, they can turn off. And if they buy one of his records – well, they must like his voice! Booth is most modest, and has little opinion of his own powers to please.

Yet he will realise a life ambition next Good Friday when he sings in **The Messiah** at the Royal Albert Hall, with Malcolm Sargent and the Royal Choral Society. He is the most versatile of singers, his repertoire ranging from the lightest of light songs to ballads, lieder, musical comedy, operas, and oratorios.

He says that he sings now as he did as a boy of eight, and that he has never had occasion to alter his method of production. He regards the late G J Bennett, who shaped his voice at Lincoln, as the best possible teacher he could have encountered. Every day for four and a half years Bennett drilled Booth. What Bennett taught has stuck. Richard Wassell had the job of transforming the boyish soprano into his present tenor voice, and Booth is as grateful to him as he is to Bennett.

November 1935
Richard Tauber has made two records in English from the film **Heart's Desire**, which should sell in thousands. The singer has complete command of his voice and is always a pleasure to hear. His English has definitely improved, despite his "I *gave* it to you now" and the songs are sufficiently different to prevent boredom. R020286 has *Let Me Awaken Your Heart* and *Vienna, City of My Dreams*; R020287, *My World is Gold Because You Love Me* and *All Hope is Ended*. All are by Tauber and Clifford Grey except *Vienna*, which is by Lockton and Rudolf Sieczynski, and reminds one of Afrique's brilliant impersonation of Tauber on a recent Decca record... If, however, you want the songs all on one record, you will find them excellently sung by Webster Booth on HMVB8385 (2/6). This *Vocal Gems* has the support of a chorus and orchestra.

December 1935
Olive Groves, Effie Atherton, Webster Booth and Stuart Robertson (1901-1958) in the **Co-optimists Medley** HMV 2800 keep bright green a memory which was in no danger (oi!) of gangrene, and the Command Performance records will delight the older and better of us.

January 1936

Webster Booth sings Logan's *Pale Moon* and Posford's *The World is Mine Tonight* on HMV B8393 (2/6). Mr Posford is known for his music in BBC shows, and in this song proves that he can beat Vienna at its own game. Both these records have orchestral accompaniments and are excellently recorded.

Roger Wimbush.

February 1936

Mr John Elton's article *The Future of Screen Opera* in your January number was most encouraging, but I cannot help feeling that certain important points demand a fuller discussion. Mr Elton quotes me as saying that the filming of opera has no future, and since it was impossible for me to enlarge on this view while reviewing the record in question, I beg the hospitality of your columns to put one or two points before your readers.

… The only past history, that is in any sense relevant is the film of **Carmen** associated with Dr Sargent, and that of **Faust**, featuring Anne Ziegler and Webster Booth, and which was, I understand, scrapped as soon as it was made. Historically, then, there is little evidence…

Roger Wimbush, Pinner, Middlesex.

March 1936

Singing Stars

Now for some of the singers of these songs that you will see in the films.

Friederich Feher, who has written the music for the film **The Robber Symphony**, conducts the orchestra while Webster Booth sings **Serenata** and **Romance** (HMV BD405). This record was issued last month but was received too late for review in our February issue; it is worth hearing if you have overlooked it in your survey of the past month's output.

April 1936

For weaker digestions, we have Webster Booth in two recordings, and I am delighted to find this singer taking his place with older favourites. Cadman's popular *At Dawning* and Forster's *Mifanwy* are on HMV B8413 (2/6) and are exactly what you would expect. But in Léhar's *Stay with Me For Ever* from **Giuditta**, Mr Booth shows us what he can do when he wants, and makes me hope that this voice will be given a chance with bigger music. He also gives a sparkling performance of *Vienna, City of My Dreams*, by Sieczynski, which I hail as the best English version. These are on HMV B8421 (2/6).

May 1936

The Robber Symphony

The Queen's Hall was pretty well filled on April 16th for the private performance of Dr. Feher's film " The Robber Symphony "; and a good part of the floor space was occupied by the London Symphony Orchestra, which played a long overture and sat silent in the darkness during the showing of the much longer film. Two and a half hours was fairly long and led perhaps to a certain *malaise* among the musicians and the film-goers in the audience.

Whether the high reputation of Frederick Feher (whose Dr. Caligari is a classic and who wrote the music and scenario of "The Robber Symphony," directed the filming, and made the whole thing into a family affair) and the prestige and energy of Messrs. Chappell & Co., who co-operated with Concordia Films Ltd. in launching this Queen Mary of the film world, will bring success with the general public, remains to be proved. But it is at the very least a gallant as well as an ambitious effort to set a new and higher standard, and there are passages of great beauty, of fantastic wit and of excellent device that will live in the memory.

Webster Booth recorded two of his songs from the film, *Romance* and *Serenata* (H.M.V. BD405), which were reviewed

in March (page 423), and described some of his experiences in the Austrian Alps scenes to W. S. Meadmore in our November number (page 227).

June 1936
Webster Booth, fresh from his triumphs in Handel's **Messiah**, revives Herbert's *Ah! Sweet Mystery of Life*, ending with an extraordinary piece of *white* singing. The reverse contains a reticent performance of *Say that You are Mine* by Lockton and Kerrich. (HMV B8435)

July 1936
Webster Booth sings *Sweet Melody of Night* and *My Love and I*, from the film **Give Us This Night**, on HMV B8442, and I daresay all but the most ardent Kiepura fans will prefer this version.

September 1936
Webster Booth is a little off colour this month in two songs by May and Feiner, *I'm All Alone* and *I'll Wait for You*, both with orchestra on HMV B8476 (2S. 6d.), but this does not detract from the fact that Mr Booth is probably the finest light tenor before the public to-day.

November 1936
Webster Booth contributes *Serenade in the Night* (Bixio, Cherubini and Kennedy), and *The Way You Look Tonight* (Fields and Kern), on HMV B8498 (2/6).

December 1936
This Year of Theatreland, 1936, has, as its name suggests, a large field for exploration and Janet Lind and Webster Booth accompanied by an unnamed orchestra make the most of it. **Anything Goes, Follow the Sun, This'll Make You Whistle**, and **Careless Rapture** are some of the shows explored by these two charming songsters on HMV C2867.

January 1937
Webster Booth is heard in a medley of tunes from the Tauber film, **Land without Music**, assisted by an orchestra

and the Lindonel Three. I still cannot enthuse over the music, but Mr Booth sings better than ever. (HMV B8520, 2/6).

February 1937
Webster Booth provides a reflective interlude with two little songs that are already on many people's lips, Rizzi's *A Song for You and Me* and Strachey's *Moon of Romance*. Jack Strachey will be remembered for his work in the monthly broadcast revues, and as the composer of the *These Foolish Things*. Mr Booth's lyrical tenor suits these ditties like a glove, while a small orchestra lends its support (HMV B8527, 2/6).

March 1937
Selections and Medleys
Excerpts from two shows current in London open the cabaret this month. First we have HMV C2890, which, incidentally, arrived too late for a February notice, and here we have an excellent team of vocalists (Janet Lind, Magda Neeld and Webster Booth) singing chosen songs from Cochran's **Home and Beauty Coronation Revue**. No doubt many have heard some of the tunes over the air, but none that I have heard so far are so clearly and ably presented as on this disc.

April 1937
Gradually Webster Booth is finding his rightful place as a member of the solo quartet in our concert halls, when the choral masterpieces are given. Only the other day a severe critic of English singing singled out Mr Booth as one of the very few elect. On records he (or is it his public?) remains content with trifles. *A Bird Sang in the Rain* is by Haydn Wood, and shows how a composer who knows his job can make a pleasant song out of the slenderest material. *Undivided*, by Sievier and Thayer, is obvious, though pleasant enough. The record is interesting as contrasting the

craftsman with the factory. Performance and recording immaculate (HMV B8545, 2/6).

May 1937
Stuart Robertson, Garda Hall, Webster Booth and Sam Costa with chorus and orchestra all contribute to a record called **Theatreland at Coronation Time**, a somewhat sanguine title, since already one of the shows represented has been withdrawn. However, the popularity of **The Vagabond King** outlives any West End production, while the record contains excellent performances of songs from **Home and Beauty**, **Swing Along**, **Balalaika** and others. Mr Booth sings gloriously, Mr Robertson defiantly, Miss Hall charmingly, while Mr Costa contributes a fleeting reminiscence of a more sophisticated and yet oh so simple entertainment. (HMV C2903, 4/-)

December 1937

Webster Booth gives us this month a further instalment of "Songs that have sold a million," in which he is joined by **Dorothy Clarke** and **Foster Richardson,** that stalwart of old Zonophone days. This time the millionaires are: The Rosary, Sifter Threads among the gold, Ali, sweet mystery of life, God send you back to me, For you alone, Homing, Parted and Trees (telescoped into one verse). (H.M.V., C3050, 4s.) Then there is a Medley of Serenades entitled "Beneath her Window" and including serenades by Drigo, Toselli, Heykens, Schubert, Di Capua and Moszkowski with Serenade in the Night, thrown in to represent our own day. Only three of these are sung. **Walter Goehr** conducts the orchestra, and **Herbert Dawson** is at the organ (H.M.V., C3051, 4S.).

February 1938
I am pretty certain that Carroll Gibbons and the Savoy Hotel Orpheans have done little that is superior in either tone, colour or presentation to their selection from Gershwin's operetta **Porgy and Bess**. Not all the credit is theirs for both Anne Ziegler and Webster Booth put in some good work as

vocalists (Columbia DX824). Booth's singing of *It Ain't Necessarily so* is an outstanding feature of this disc.

Two more numbers from the film, **Firefly**, *Sympathy* and *Giannina Mia* – from the film receive careful treatment on both Decca F6562 and Rex 9201; *Carlo Santana's Accordion Band and *Prima Scala's Accordion Band are the respective executants. There is little to choose between them so hear them both.

*Both these bands were fronted by Harry Bidgood!

Snow White and the Seven Dwarfs, film selection, Orchestra of the Merry Men, with Nora Savage, Webster Booth and vocal quartet, directed by George Scott Wood. Part 1: *I'm Wishing*, *One Song*, *With a Smile and a Song*. Part 2: *Whistle While You Work*, *Heigh-ho*, *Dwarfs' Yodel Song*, *Some Day My Prince will Come* Columbia DX832

November 1938

SONGS

As readers will remember the hope has more than once been expressed in this column that **Webster Booth** might be given a chance in some music worthy of his gifts, and so it is with very great pleasure that I draw attention to a recording, held over from last month, of two operatic arias sung in English. These are *Your tiny hand is frozen* from Puccini's " La Bohème " and *The Flower Song* from Bizet's " Carmen," which can be taken as a centenary tribute to the composer, who was born on October 25th, 1838. I rate this a very fine recording in every respect, with the exception of the singer's *falsetto* in the Bizet. The voice is fresh and radiant, and the phrasing displays a musician of taste. There are excellent accompaniments by the **London Philharmonic Orchestra** under **Warwick Braithwaite** and the recording is flawless. A second record containing the two well-known tenor arias from Puccini's " Tosca " is already on the

way, though too late for review in this issue, and we can confidently hope that Mr. Booth is engaged on a series of operatic recordings in English on plum label, an enterprise which harks back to the prodigious days ten years ago. It is an enterprise that has my very best wishes. (H.M.V., C3030, 4s.)

December 1938

Webster Booth gives us this month a further instalment of "Songs that have sold a million," in which he is joined by **Dorothy Clarke** and **Foster Richardson**, that stalwart of old Zonophone days. This time the millionaires are: The Rosary, Sifter Threads among the gold, Ah, sweet mystery of life, God send you back to me, For you alone, Homing, Parted and Trees (telescoped into one verse). (H.M.V., C3050, 4s.) Then there is a Medley of Serenades entitled "Beneath her Window" and including serenades by Drigo, Toselli, Heykens, Schubert, Di Capua and Moszkowski with Serenade in the Night, thrown in to represent our own day. Only three of these are sung. **Walter Goehr** conducts the orchestra, and **Herbert Dawson** is at the organ (H.M.V., C3051, 4S.).

January 1939
MASTERPIECES of 1938

Frank Titterton	Erl King	Decca F6534
Peter Dawson	Two Grenadiers	HMV B8695
Norman Walker	Holbrooke excerpts	Decca X176
Nan Maryska	Alleluia	HMV B8728
Raymond Newell	The Devil of the Flora Dee	Columbia DB1759
Lyons Mixed Chorus	Trois Chansons	Columbia DX849
Sydney MacEwan	Sacrament	Parlophone R2526
Tino Rossi	Aubade	Columbia DB1792
Nancy Evans	Gurney Songs	Decca K889-90
Richard Tauber	English Rose	Parlophone RO2042
Webster Booth	Flower Song	HMV C3030
Millicent Phillips	Il Bacio	Parlophone R2589

February 1939

> **Webster Booth** (tenor) with **L. Collingwood** conducting the
> orchestra : **Woman is fickle** (La donna è mobile) and
> **This one or that one** (Questa o quella), both from
> **Rigoletto** (Verdi) ; sung in English. H.M.V., B8829
> (10 in., 3s.).

I am glad that this record by Mr. Booth has come my way,
as I had begun to think that my colleague R.W. would get
them all. It was hardly to be expected that the singer should
achieve anything strikingly original with such well-worn
favourites as *Questa o quella* and *La donna è mobile* ; what could be
hoped for was the pleasant easy-flowing delivery of both arias
in a manner suggestive of a care-free, gay philanderer. This is
quite satisfactorily achieved ; moreover, the singer has chosen
to sing in English and most of his words are easily caught at a
first hearing. Hence the record, which is technically very
satisfactory, can be warmly commended.

Since H.M.V. are interesting themselves in opera in English,
it is perhaps permissible to ask for English titles to be chosen for
their recordings on a uniform plan. We have had " first-line "
and descriptive titles. Here we encounter " literal translation "
titles ; is there any need for them?

March 1939
Ealing and Hanwell Gramophone Society.
After the interval, the remainder of the programme was
devoted to selections from **La Bohème** – Webster Booth
and Marta Eggerth playing a prominent part. We realised
from Tubiana what an attachment there was to that old coat.
Parting from it with reluctance, even for the sake of Mimi,
seemed to be the impression.

April 1939
Readers will forgive me for taking a special pride in the
current recordings made by Webster Booth because for
months I pleaded for such records. Now that they have
come, they are being appraised by eminent critics in a
variety of journals. Our own HFVL showed the keenest

delight in reviewing some recent operatic excerpts, and I was glad to have my opinion endorsed by one who has never let a shoddy piece of work get past him. People who are in the habit of attending concerts at the Albert Hall will be glad to have Mr Booth's new record of the recitative *Comfort Ye* and the aria *Ev'ry Valley shall be Exalted* from Handel's **Messiah**. Considering that oratorio is still the Englishman's special delight it is strange how little of it gets recorded except in albums which the average enthusiast, generally an industrial worker, can ill afford. I do not find this singing particularly inspired, but it is a careful performance which will please many and offend none. Since my copy is an advance pressing I am unable to say who is responsible for the accompaniments, but they are adequately done. (HMV C3087 4/-). If Messrs Dawson and Booth are both going to get busy on these lines, we shall have an exciting time ahead of us.

May 1939
Following his recording from **Messiah**, Webster Booth excels all previous records in two extracts from Mendelssohn's **Elijah**: *If with All Your Hearts* and *Then Shall the Righteous*. The voice sounds much fuller than last month, and if this is an indication that we may expect good modern recordings or oratorio it has my blessing. This is an exceedingly fine record. (HMV C3095, 4/-).

June 1939

Writing above of Dame Ethel Smyth's work brings to mind the great success of that composer's " Wreckers " a few weeks back at Sadler's Wells, and that, in turn, leads us to a record—issued in December last—of Joan Cross and Webster Booth in the " Miserere " from " Il Trovatore " and the " O soave fanciulla " duet from Act I of " La Bohème." Rendering, accompaniment (Sadler's Wells Orchestra under Lawrance Collingwood), and recording are all excellent, and I much prefer this disc to the more recent record by Wells artistes of the Trio from " Faust," which has been awkwardly " cut." My personal preference is for opera sung in its native tongue, and that is my only complaint against these two records : the same factor will probably weigh the scales just as heavily on the opposite side for many gramophiles, however, since a dealer friend assures me that a large section of the record-buying public prefers its opera sung in English. For all such collectors, H.M.V. C3053 (4s.), with the two duets, will become an immediate necessity. Here I think is a fitting place to pay tribute to the magnificent work for music in England being carried out at Sadler's Wells where, without pretension, artistes and all concerned are working for the love of their art. To British composers and singers not least of all, knowledge of this work must be a great encouragement, and those of us who some years ago predicted a great future for Webster Booth, at a time when he was singing vocal refrains in light orchestral recordings, will the more heartily congratulate him on his deserved success this year at the Wells.

July 1939

Here is a real winner : **Webster Booth** singing Geehl's *For You Alone* and D'Hardelot's *Because* on H.M.V. B8920 (3s.). This is most certainly a nap, and will sell for years. Two of the most popular songs in our language, sung by one of our few great tenors and magnificently recorded with an orchestral accompaniment conducted by **Clifford Greenwood.** Mr. Booth sings these all out, just as Tod Slaughter plays the melodrama of the period. It is the only way to do it, and in both cases it comes off triumphantly. I remember a broadcast from Vienna of " Die Fledermaus," in which Alfred Piccaver sang *For You Alone* in English during the ball scene and brought down the house. Mr. Booth shows us that these are songs to *sing*.

September 1939

Webster **Booth**

"The Immortal Hour" is now being revived by the Covent Garden Touring Company which will play it in the provinces during the autumn. Its most famous number is this lovely "Faery Song" which Webster Booth has made one of his finest records to date. One of the features is the delightful Harp accompaniment (here played by John Cockerill). "The English Rose" is one of the best known songs from Edward German's comic opera "Merrie England." This is, of course, sung with full orchestral accompaniment.

The Faery Song ("The Immortal Hour")
The English Rose ("Merrie England")
B8947—3/-

October 1939

SONGS

Alan Murray's *I'll walk beside you* is having a vogue. **Webster Booth** sings it with *Macushla* on H.M.V. B8968 (3s.) and gives to each ballad the polish and fervour that he deems to be their due. Boulanger's *My Prayer* is also having a vogue and here it is sung with his distinctive ease by **Alfred Piccaver** who adds *Love's Serenade* by Hayes-Kurtz-Mills (Brunswick 02816, 3s.). Thirdly, the choice of **Dennis Noble** this month is Sanderson's *Until* and Barker's *The Organ Blower* (H.M.V. B8970, 3s.) which suits his beautiful baritone voice.

SONGS TOO LATE FOR REVIEW

The Gospel Singer (Roland Robson): *Lead kindly light* and *Abide with Me* (Col. FB2309). **Harold Williams:** *Lords of the Air* and *We'll remember* (Col. DB1892). **Nelson Eddy:** *Four Indian Love Lyrics* (Col. LB57-8). **John McCormack:** *Bless this house* and *Bird songs at eventide* (H.M.V. DA1712). **Webster Booth:** *Ave Maria* (Bach-Gounod) and *Agnus Dei* (Bizet), with L.P.O. under **Wynn Reeves** and organ by **Herbert Dawson** (H.M.V. B8990). **Webster Booth** and **Dennis Noble:** *Excelsior* and *Watchman what of the night* (H.M.V. C3124). **Webster Booth** with organ by **Herbert Dawson:** *The Lost Chord* and *Handel's Largo* (H.M.V. C3130). **Dennis Noble,** piano by **Gerald Moore:** *Nirvana* and *The Trumpeter* (H.M.V. C3125). **Sadler's Wells Chorus and Orchestra** conducted by **Warwick Braithwaite:** *Barcarolle from " Tales of Hoffmann "* and *Easter Hymn from " Cavalleria Rusticana "* (H.M.V. C3126). **Light Opera Company** under **Isidore Godfrey:** *Vocal Gems from " The Mikado "* (H.M.V. C3128). **Kentucky Minstrels:** *Bless this house* and *Passing by* (H.M.V. BD761) ; *The Star of Bethlehem* (H.M.V. BD763). **Uncle Mac's Christmas Carols** with **Leslie Woodgate** and **St. Brandon's C.D.S. Choir** (H.M.V. BD767-9). **The Cathedral Quartet:** *O come all ye faithful* and *Hark the herald angels sing* (H.M.V. BD777).

1/2 - NINETEEN-FORTIES

January 1940

Webster Booth has sung Liszt's **Liebestraum**. Like the Petrarch Sonnets in the Italian Year of Pilgrimage, the three **Liebestraum** nocturnes, of which this is the third, were originally songs. In some ways it is a pity that we have that unforgettable record by Meta Seinemeyer, made just before she died and accompanied by the man she married almost on her death-bed – "Oh, love me as long as you can, for soon you will stand by the grave and mourn" – so runs the song, but not in the setting used by Mr Booth, obviously taken from Liszt's piano arrangement, whereas Seinemeyer went to the original. However, the singing is immaculate, and Tosti's **Goodbye** is truly magnificent on the reverse.

    The other record is of Webster Booth singing the Largo in full with recitative. This is important, for despite all the existing recordings, I do not know of one which includes this. B8990, backed by the Bach-Gounod **Ave Maria**. I know that sounds awful, and in some ways perhaps it is. Personally I have never seen the objections to Gounod's alleged sacrilege, but I am inclined to agree that this is too much. Wynn Reeves conducts the LPO for the **Largo**; Herbert Dawson plays the organ for **The Lost Chord** (Booth). Here is the famous song in its operatic setting. Magnificently sung and recorded. It seems strange to us now that this comes from a comic opera! (HMV C3130, 4/-)

February 1940

To the Editor of THE GRAMOPHONE

May I through the medium of your paper ask The Gramophone Company to give us some more plum-label operatic records by British singers ?

At the present time they appear to have the services of four singers in particular, whose voices record well and whose popularity must surely help the ever important commercial standpoint. In addition they can all be relied upon to give performances of a high standard of excellence.

I refer to Joan Cross, Edith Coates, Webster Booth and Dennis Noble. So far the operatic recordings by these artists have been of " safe " selections from the most popular scores. Without dashing to the other extreme of excessively modern and presumably non-commercial works, there are many solos, duets, trios, etc., which I would much like recorded by these singers, a desire which, I am sure, is shared by many other opera lovers in this country.

I give below a list of a few suggestions which would, in my opinion, make a good start.

Joan Cross and Edith Coates : Elsa-Ortrude duet, "Lohengrin." Evening Prayer duet, " Hansel and Gretel." Orpheus-Eurydice duet, " Orpheus." Lakmé-Mallika duet, " Lakmé."

Joan Cross and Dennis Noble : Duet Giorgetta-Michele, " Il Tabarro." Duet Nedda-Silvio, " Pagliacci." Duet Tatiana-Onegin, " Eugen Onegin." Duet Leonora-di Luna, " Il Trovatore." Duet Norina-Malatesta, " Don Pasquale."

Joan Cross and Webster Booth : Duet Manon-Des-Grieux,

" Manon Lescaut." Duet Micaela-Don José, " Carmen." Duet from final scene, " Andrea Chenier."

Webster Booth and Dennis Noble : Duet Nadir-Zurga, " The Pearlfishers."

Cross, Coates and Booth : Trio from last act of " Tales of Hoffmann."

Cross, Coates, Booth and Noble : " Spinning " Quartette, " Marta." " Good-night " Quartette, " Marta."

London, N.W.8.   NEVILLE WALLIS.

Webster Booth challenges comparison with Fleta by singing *Ay, Ay, Ay,* which he does beautifully, and the same applies to Tosti's *Ideale* on HMV B9009 (3/-). Warwick Braithwaite conducts the orchestra.

Clifford Greenwood takes charge for the new duet record by Mr Booth and Anne Ziegler. This is of *I'll See You Again* from Noel Coward's **Bitter Sweet** and *Wanting You* from Sigmund Romberg's **The New Moon**. This is charming, and the Coward includes the delightful verse. These musical comedy duets are a welcome addition to the lists. (HMV B8996)

Following the **Mikado** selection, we now have **The Gondoliers** - vocal gems there from sung by the Light Opera Company under Isidore Godfrey. We recognise George Baker, Webster Booth and Dennis Noble, and we see increasing signs that Sullivan's operatic music is soon to be worthily performed. We shall learn that soubrettes cannot sing music written for dramatic sopranos and that the orchestral writing of a master requires rehearsal.

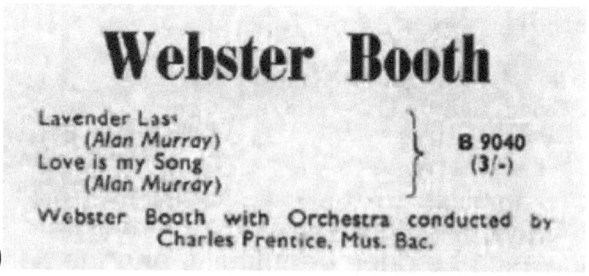

May 1940

Noel Eadie, Nancy Evans, Webster Booth and Dennis Noble :
Vocal Gems from" Carmen" (Bizet). H.M.V. C3143 (12 in., 4s.).

" Vocal Gems " is hardly a fair description of what is really a dramatic
potting of the opera. The excerpts are cleverly knit. and the music
progresses without any blatant jerks. All the favourite bits are here, and
the finale is especially well done, the singers really getting inside their
parts. Ample support is given by the Sadler's Wells Chorus and Orchestra
under Warwick Braithwaite.

July 1940
Songs
Webster Booth and Anne Ziegler continue to record extracts from musical comedy and on HMV B9060 (3/-) sing *Deep in My Heart* from **The Student Prince** (Romberg) and *Fold Your Wings* from Ivor Novello's **Glamorous Night**, while Mr Booth adds *The Serenade* from **The Student Prince** coupled with *Oh, Maiden, My Maiden* from **Frederica** on B9058 (3/-).

December 1940

It must surely be obvious to all readers that the latest English
recording is miles ahead of the best American which is invariably
harsh, ill-balanced, with vile string tone, and amongst the worst
of these must be included the records made by the aristocratic
Toscanini the labels of which seem to blush for very shame.

In conclusion I would like to mention three H.M.V. plum
label vocal records which in their way are every bit as outstanding as the Beecham "España" and these are the four
operatic arias by Dennis Noble and Handel's "Rest" and
Sullivan's "Lost Chord" by Webster Booth.
Dunster.   MOORE ORR

April 1941

Webster Booth (tenor) : Gerald Moore (piano) : The Mountains o' Mourne (French-Collisson) : (*a*) A Ballynure Ballad (arr. Hughes) ; (*b*) Trottin' to the Fair (Graves-Stanford). H.M.V., B9164 (10 in., 3s. 8d.).

Constant comparison with the past can be very wearisome, but it would be affectation not to speak of Plunket Greene's inimitable singing of " Trottin' to the Fair." Mr. Booth sings it well and, as in the other two songs, his diction is exceptionally good : but he does not fully convey the point of Molly's " didn't answer no," nor does he get the delightful speaking tone into his voice that the older artist used. I am rather tired of that unsophisticated Irishman who expected to find London paved with gold and so far as I'm concerned he can stay in the " Mountains of Mourne " : but I welcome Mr. Booth's singing of the " Ballynure Ballad." Will not this excellent artist cast his net more widely please ? Mr. Moore's accompanying is a joy and the recording is good.

August 1941
Anne Ziegler and Webster Booth
Will You Remember? (**Sweethearts**) (Romberg); *Love's Garden of Roses* (Rutherford, Haydn Wood) HMV B9177 (10" 3/8)
These singers have established themselves as the most popular duettists of the light, melodious school. There is very little that one can say about these favourite numbers except that they are done very well indeed, and will bring joy to the many Ziegler-Booth fans.

September 1941

(Ross-Schubert, arr. Clutsam). H.M.V. B9202 (50 in., 3s. 8d.).

Although the purists shuddered at the thought of Schubert's music being lifted to form the basis of a musical comedy, "Lilac Time" has been an unqualified success, and has brought much of Schubert's loveliest vocal music to the ears of many who would not have heard it in its original form. Anne Ziegler and Webster Booth give a delightful performance of these two duets, which can be heartily recommended to all who have a liking for melody.

1941

GANGWAY

Revue devised by George Black. **Music** and **Lyrics**: Harry Parr-Davies, Noel Gay, *et al.*

London Palladium, 17 December 1941

The **Cast** included:

> Webster Booth, Teddy Brown, Bebe Daniels, Roberta Huby, Ben Lyon, Tommy Trinder, Anne Ziegler

The **Programme** included:

1. So Deep Is the Night
2. My Paradise
3. There's Something About That Town (*Gay-Eyton*)
4. Swing Bugler (*Park-Campbell-Thompson*)

January 1942
Webster Booth (tenor) with orchestra: ***Star of My Soul*** (Greenbank-Jones): ***To Mary*** (Shelley-White). HMV B9244 (10", 3/6d.).

Webster Booth's admirers will like his new record. ***Star of My Soul*** has one of those easy, singable melodies that were often to be found in the older musical plays. ***To Mary*** is a good example of Maude Valerie White's clean vocal line, and the two songs make excellent record companions.

Webster Booth (tenor) with orchestra : **Song of the Vagabonds** (Hooker-Friml) **One Alone** (Mandel-Romberg). H.M.V. B9255 (to ins., 3s. id.).

The " Song of the Vagabonds," in which the poet Villon hurls raging defiance at the Duke of Burgundy, depended very greatly in the show itself on the effective support of a large and defiant chorus. Webster Booth does without a chorus in this record, but he lets himself go so valiantly that he is a host in himself. By contrast, in " One Alone," now an established favourite, he takes the languorous, yearning phrases in his smoothest and easiest style. As usual, his words are beautifully clear.

WEBSTER BOOTH

| Star of my Soul ; To Mary | - | - | B 9244 |
| Trees ; Song of Songs | - | - | B 9205 |

with The Hallé Orchestra

| A wand'ring Minstrel I | - | -⎫ | |
| Take a pair of Sparkling Eyes | - ⎬ | | C 3261 |

ANNE ZIEGLER AND WEBSTER BOOTH

So deep is the Night ; My Paradise		B 9247
When we are Married	-	-⎫	
The Keys of Heaven -	-	- ⎬	B 9226

There is a wide choice of songs and singers, of which we can only mention two songs from the **Savoy Operas** recorded by Mr Webster Booth, two Scottish songs sung by Mr Sydney MacEwan, and two attractive boy's solos (Master Denis Wright).

February 1942
Anne Ziegler and Charles Forwood (piano): *Slumber Song* (Schumann, arr. Carroll): *A Song in the Night* (Mortimer/Loughborough). HMV B9243 (10", 3/6d.).

Schumann wrote hosts of tiny pieces for the piano, and a good many have been arranged for the voice or for other instruments. The *Schlummerlied* (*Slumber Song*) is one of these, and with its gentle rocking accompaniment and simple melody offers no difficulty to Anne Ziegler. The other side contains a typical and not very striking trifle about a nightingale singing in a wood. Just another bird song at twilight, so to speak.

December 1942
Extract from letter
Where'er you walk, by Pope. The words sung by Mr Webster Booth on C3305 are identical with those always associated with this music. My copy of the score distinctly states that they are by Congreve, and if further confirmation is required it will be found of p. 141 of *Handel*, in Dent's Master Musician Series, edited by Eric Blom. ROBERT F NATHAN

Webster Booth (tenor) With instrumental quintet: (a) **Down by the Pond** (From "Now We are Six"): **Chris.. topher Robin is Saying His Prayers** (From" When We were very Young ") and **Sneezies** (" Now We are Six ") **Buckingham Palace** (" When We were very Young"). H.MV. B9304 (io in., 45. 8d.).

There is, I feel, a tendency to take A. A. Milne's Christopher Robin poems too seriously, and Webster Booth's singing of four of Fraser-Simson's tuneful settings deepens the impression. They are just clever trifles, and ask for a light, almost humorous handling. Webster Booth could not sing them otherwise than tunefully, and his diction, is perfect, but the spontaneous touch is lacking, and at times he sounds self-conscious. The recording is very good, and of the four I preferred Sneezles.

October 1942
Webster Booth (tenor) and Hallé Orchestra (Braithwaite): *Where'er You Walk*, (Pope/Handel)*: Be Thou Faithful unto Death* (Mendelssohn) HMV C3305 (12", 5/9)
His easy style of production, perfectly clear diction and absolutely sure pitch are just the essentials for oratorio solos. And as so few singers possess them in equal measure that I place Webster Booth as almost unique in that respect. His new record, with its rich orchestral

accompaniment, has no hint of war-time austerities, and gives some of his best singing to date.

Handel turned away from opera and devoted himself to oratorio. **Semele** was written in 1743, the year following the **Messiah**, and the thin division between Handel's operas and oratorios, or many of them, at any rate, may be gathered from the fact that it was announced at different times in the *General Advertiser* as "**Semele**, after the manner of an Opera," and "**Semele**, after the manner of an Oratorio." The last revival seems to have been at Cambridge in 1878. Where're you walk has always been popular with tenors and the record catalogues of the past thirty years show how magnetic was its attraction. Like many another Handelian aria, it is now the sole survivor from the parent work.

Mendelssohn's vocal music, particularly from the oratorios, has suffered an almost total eclipse, and I should not be surprised if the fine Cavatina *Be thou faithful unto death* is almost unknown to the present generation of record buyers. Here is a chance of making its acquaintance under the most favourable circumstances. H.D.R.

November 1942
Webster Booth (tenor) and Hallé Orchestra (Braithwaite): *Prize Song*, **Die Meistersingers** (Wagner); *All Hail, Thou Dwelling*, **Faust** (Gounod) HMV C3309 (12", 5/9)
Two excellent and sensitively sung recordings of these famous arias. Such effortless lyrical singing gives great pleasure. It never gives one that sympathetic tightness of throat induced by some tenors. One misses, of course, the chorus and Eva's lovely interjection in *The Prize Song*, but there is much to be thankful for. I hope Mr Booth will go on extending his operatic repertoire and make it include the many lovely arias in rarely performed operas. A.R.

1943

Webster Booth (tenor): **Liverpool Phil- harmonic Orchestra** (Sargent) **Speak for Me to My Lady** (11 mio tesoro), **Mine be her Burden** (Dalla sua pace) from **"Don Giovanni"** (Da Ponti-Dent-Mozart). H.M.V. C3372 (to- ins., 6s. 7d)

It is nice to find Webster Booth going along the road of operatic salvation. He does well with these two testing arias, which he sings with conviction, warmth of tone, and good taste: if not with the ultimate refinement of style I hoFe he may one day acquire. The Liverpool Philharmonic, under. Sargent, provide adequate accompaniments and the recording is good.

February 1943

Tuneful singing and clearness of words are always to be expected from these popular artists, and adds greatly to the enjoyment of these duets. Anne Ziegler and Webster Booth have long been stage partners, and will, I am told, be appearing together in a revival of " The Vagabond King." The accompaniments are good and the recording first class.

May 1943

Three male singers, two tenors and a bari-tone, present a choice of short songs on 10in. disks. Mr. Richard Tauber sings Grieg with orchestra and Mr. Webster Booth sings familiar songs of Mendelssohn and Schubert with piano. Both these singers are too close to the microphone. Mr. Roy Henderson uses that tricky instrument to retain the intimacy of Stanford's " The Fairy Lough " and the excitement of the ·same composer's " The Pibroch."

August 1943

Mr J Arthers, Sunbury, asks for records of Mary Jarred and William Parsons. Mary Jarred has recorded for Columbia and on an HMV record. He thinks the British Council should sponsor **Dream of Gerontius** with above and Webster Booth.

October 1943

Webster Booth (tenor), **Hubert Green- slade** (piano) : **Temple Bells** and **Less than the Dust** from **Four Indian Love Lyrics** (Hope-Woodforde-Finden). H.M.V. 139342 (to in., 5s. 4id-)

It is just about forty years ago since the late Amy Woodforde-Finden's "Four Indian Love Lyrics" first reached the grateful ears of ballad concert habitues. To judge by their perennial appearance in record lists they have lost none of their appeal. Webster Booth is the latest of a long line of Indian lovers, with a really excellent record of the first two of the songs, Temple Bells and Less than the Dust. They lie easily within his range and he sings them with an ease of style and clarity of diction that leave nothing to be desired. It is also good to hear the original piano accompaniments clearly played. An improvement, in my opinion, on some of the orchestral versions with which drawing room songs of this type are frequently overloaded.

November 1943

Anne Ziegler (soprano) : **Webster Booth** (tenor) with Orchestra : **Without Your Love** " The Dubarry " (Leigh-Millocker-Mackeben) : **What is Done** " Lilac Domino " (Smith-Cuvillier). H.M.V. B9326 (10 ins., 5s. 4½d.).

These popular singers have already made a considerable series of love duets from the best musical comedies, and the latest are well up to standard, quite pretty, and with some brilliant work for the soprano. They will possibly be new to many who like light and melodious records, which is an additional recommendation. Anne Ziegler and Webster Booth are at present starring in the revival of " The Vagabond King."

Webster Booth (tenor), Dennis Noble (baritone), Hallé Orchestra (BraithWaite): In a Coupé, "La Bohéme" (Pinkerton-Puccini). Gwen Catley (soprano): Dearest Name, "Rigoletto" (Levy-Verdi). H.M.V. C3369 (12 in., 6s. 7d.).

It was an excellent idea to start this recording at the opening of the last act of Bohéme, and none the less so if it was dictated by purely practical reasons. Both artists seem thoroughly in the skin of their parts and I much liked the unabashed sentimentality of their singing. Diction, too, is good, and so is the orchestral accompaniment both in tone and balance. The degree of reverberation is right. A most enjoyable and very well sung, played> and recorded excerpt.

Webster Booth (tenor) : **Hubert Green-slade** (piano) : **Kashmiri Song** and **Till I Wake** from **Four Indian Love Lyrics** (Hope-Woodforde-Finden). H.M.V. B9343 (10 in., 5s. 4½d.).
With this record, Webster Booth completes his rendering of the *Four Indian Love Lyrics*, and he does them very well indeed. I recommend this (and its predecessor) wholeheartedly to any, if there be any, who have not already acquired any of the existing versions. Once again I must compliment Mr. Booth on his diction, which is a model of clarity.

Another 10" in a lighter vein gives two duets from films, sung by Anne Ziegler and Webster Booth, *Only a Rose*, from the film **Vagabond King**, and *You, Just You*, from the film **Wild Violets**.
There are a number of attractive vocal records, all 10", among the month's publications, Webster Booth, with Gerald Moore at the piano, in **Come Back My Love**, and *Will You Go With Me?*

January 1944

From Miss JOAN MARTIN, 53, Lake View,
    Edgware.
H.M.V.—DB2943. Italian Girl in Algiers
    (Rossini). N.Y. Phil. Symphony Orch.,
    cond. Toscanini. My favourite Rossini
    overture. Thrilling music, working up to a
    terrific climax ; a record of which one can
    never tire.
H.M.V.—B8990. Ave Maria (Bach-Gounod).
    Webster Booth. Ethereal music, exquisitely
    sung, with chorus in the background. This
    recording gives new life to a rather hackneyed
    song.
H.M.V.—C3309. Prize Song (Mastersingers).
    Another of Webster Booth's magnificent
    recordings—my favourite vocal record. The
    coupling is " All Hail thou Dwelling," also
    very fine. W.B. sings both these arias with
    great sincerity and feeling, and I think this
    is one of his best recordings.

I wish Amgot would exert its influence to secure Italian on records again. Mr Webster Booth has made an excellent record of *Il Mio Tesoro* and *Dalla Sua Pace* from **Don Giovanni** on a 12-inch HMV plum disc, but Professor Dent, with all his ingenuity, cannot make the English anything but difficult if true Mozartian grace is to be achieved. *Mine be Her Burden* is not a good substitute in sound for *Dalla Sua Pace*.

February 1944
Duet from **Madame Butterfly**, with Joan Hammond

, (12 in., 6s. 7½-d.).

On the whole an excellent recording. The balance between voices and orchestra is reasonably good and the singing itself is impassioned and eager. Miss Hammond lets herself go a little too early on and the difficult phrase "as you would love a baby" (which Butterfly can't really have meant !) defeats her as it has defeated most sopranos who sing in English. But for the rest it is good to hear a real weight of tone and a voice which can give us a sense of climax, albeit a voice that needs more discipline. Webster Booth sings admirably throughout and the recording is good, though probably hard on small instruments.

March 1944

Webster Booth (tenor): **Liverpool Philharmonic Orchestra** (Sargent): **Heavenly Aida** (Ghizlanzoni-Kenney-Verdi): **On with the Motley** ("**Pagliacci**") (Weatherley-Leoncavallo). Conductor, Cameron. Sung in English. H.M.V. C3379 (12 ins., 6s. 7½d.).

The only fault to be found in this fine pair of recordings is the over-amplification of the voice, but that is unlikely to worry anyone who has not heard the artist in the flesh. Thank goodness we are given the recitatives preceding each air and also the whole of the orchestral epilogue to "On with the Motley." This has never before,

surely, been carried so far or been so well played. Another reason for thankfulness is that Mr. Booth does not try to emulate Italian hysteria as Canio, and delivers himself, as Radames, of a really soft high B flat at the close of the aria. The ringing trumpets must, for their part, be commended. The singing, playing and recording are really first-rate.

April 1944

Anne Ziegler (soprano): **Webster Booth**
(tenor) with orchestra. **Indian Love
Call** (Harback-Hammerstein-Friml):
Barcarolle from "**Tales of Hoffman**" (Offenbach). H.M.V. B9370
(10 in., 5s. 4½d.)

The Indian Love Call comes out very
effectively in this recording and is very
charmingly sung: but the poor Barcarolle
is absurdly messed about. You will remember that Offenbach wrote it for two
unequal voices, soprano and contralto. To
make the contralto into a tenor is to make
the composer's vocal harmony sound silly
—as it does here. Moreover the duet is too
quickly sung—or sounds so—and is lacking
in the nostalgic atmosphere which it requires.

June 1944

SONGS Webster Booth (tenor): Dennis Noble (baritone) with
Liverpool Philhar- monic Orchestra (Cameron): 'Tis The Spring of
All Invention and Fifteen My Number Is from 'The Barber of
Seville" (Natalie Macfarren-Rossini). H.M.V. C3398 (12 ins., 6s. 7d.).

This is the duet from Act 1 in which Figaro suggests to the
love-sick Count Almavira that he should dress himself up as
a soldier and feign being drunk: in this way he will more
easily gain access to Doctor Bartolo's house and, above all,
to his ward, Rosina. Figaro begins the description of his
shop on the other side of the record, *Fifteen My Number is*,
and the duet ends with the Count singing of the love in his
heart, Figaro of the money chinking in his pocket. Dennis
Noble is nearest to perfection as Figaro and is well partnered
by Webster Booth. Their florid passages are very cleanly
done, the orchestral accompaniment is excellent and
altogether this is a delightful recording. The stock translation

is replaced by one far better in every way (Professor Dent's), but I could not hear all of Webster Booth's words.

October 1944

Webster Booth (tenor): **Liverpool Phil- harmonic Orchestra** (Sargent). **Onaway ! Awake, Beloved** "Hiawatha" (Longfellow - Coleridge - Taylor). **o Vision Entrancing** "Esmeralda" (Marzials- Thomas). H.M.V. C3407 (I2ins., fis. 71d.).

There are one or two good phrases in these faded airs and at least they are vocal. "Onaway ! Awake, beloved" always seemed to me to be one of the weakest pages in Hiawatha. The loveliest and most enduring part of the cantata is surely "The death of Minehaha." Webster Booth sings both airs beautifully. The orchestral accompaniment is still not as good as it ought to be, as recorded. Those words must be emphasised because I recently received a friendly tirade of three pages about my alleged unfairness to this orchestra. I can only say—to take one instance—that if Reginald Kell, for whom I have an immense admiration, was playing the clarinet when the Delius Violin Concerto was recorded, then, so uncharacteristic was the tone, there must be something wrong with the placing of the microphone. In the recording now under review the orchestral detail is cloudy instead of clear. All teems well when the orchestra is on its own. I praised both Schubert's" Italian Overture" and John Ireland's " London Overture but I have not yet felt happy about the orchestra in its role as accompanist: as— I add again----recorded.

December 1944

Webster Booth (tenor): Liverpool Philharmonic Orchestra (Sargent): *Deeper and Deeper Still* (Recit.). *Waft Her angels* (Air). **Jephtha** (Handel). HMV C3414 (12" 6/7d).

I should be interested to know who was first responsible for linking *Deeper and Deeper Still* with *Waft Her Angels*. Certainly it was not Handel! In the score the aria is preceded by a recitative *Hide Thy Beams Thou Hated Sun* which opens Act Three of the work. Act Two ends with a chorus *How Dark are Thy Decrees*, and it is immediately before this that the recitative **Deeper and Deeper Still** comes. It is a most expressive piece of writing, and Mr Booth conveys movingly the terrible distress of Jephtha now that Israel has triumphed and, in obedience to his vow, he must sacrifice his daughter. I wish that both singer and the orchestra had more exactly observed Handel's directions.

"Oh let me whisper it to the raging winds" is marked double piano, for whisper is the operative word. But singer and orchestra, disdaining under-statement, throw in a forte to illustrate "raging." Again in the aria why should the rising phrase "far above yon azure plain "carry a crescendo to forte. If the phrase is sung crescendo to piano the effect is much more tender and moving. The strings, in fact, almost do this when they have the same phrase earlier in the aria. Some people may think such criticism niggling. I shall continue, nevertheless, to urge in and out of season that the composer's directions—where they make sense—should be implicitly obeyed. In this case the very sense of the words in the recitative demands it.

Otherwise the singer's performance is most excellent and beautiful in tone and expression. The orchestral accompaniment is good but the chording of the strings is not always precise, and why are horns and oboes scored into the aria. Handel uses only strings. The recording is good.

February 1945
Webster Booth (tenor): Gerald Moore (piano): **Come into the Garden Maud** (Tennyson-Balfe): Ernest Lush (piano): Alfredo Campoli (violin): **Morgen!** Op.27 (Berrihoff-R.Strauss). HMV. C3418 (6/7d).

A solo violin is, of course, prominent in Strauss's orchestral arrangement of **Morgen**: and one cannot really object violently to its presence in this the original version of the song, even though the composer provided only the piano accompaniment. The long held notes might easily go dead in the recording. Needless to say the violin *obbligato* is beautifully played by Campoli. (May we not hear this fine artist in some solo work: he is capable of rising to great heights?) The only fault I have to find with Webster Booth's very sensitive and well-controlled singing is the pace. I doubt if the over-all timing of the exquisite record of this song made by Elizabeth Schumann is actually any longer, but there was a deliberate application of *rubato* which seems to be missing here; and a very slight sense of hurrying just disturbs the peaceful atmosphere in which the song should move.

Over **Maud** my sympathies are with the singer. It must be difficult to work up much enthusiasm about the damsel: though as the Editor reminded us the other day, John McCormack managed it. I can't help thinking that Somervell, in his setting of these words, did well to seize on the hint given by the mention of that odd trio, flute, violin, bassoon (which, according to the poet, the roses heard all night) and so wrote a beguiling dance tune to float his Maud.

Nevertheless, Mr Booth's excellent singing of the hardy old ballad will give much pleasure. I note that Ernest Lush "returns to the microphone" in **Morgen** and that Gerald Moore is almost inaudible in the Balfe. Will someone not give the closest attention to this matter of a true balance between piano (orchestra) and voice. I heard recently the new French recording of **Pelleas**: and there again the voices are more than life-size - the orchestra a mere thread of sound. These faults easily spoil enjoyment.

August 1945
The recitative **Thy Rebuke Hath Broken His Heart** and the arioso following **Behold, and See if There be any Sorrow** are among the most moving pages of **Messiah**. The materialism of the big choruses gives place, once again, to the humanity and tenderness Handel knew so well how to express: and in such pages he comes nearest to deep religious feeling. Webster Booth, satisfactorily accompanied

by the Birmingham City Orchestra, sings expressively and well, but he should learn to avoid loudening notes just because they are higher in pitch than those that precede them. In the line "He is full of heaviness," there is no sense at all in pushing at the preposition and in "like unto His sorrow", "His" and not the first word (on the highest note) is the important one. The fact that Handel's accentuation is at fault does not absolve the singer from correcting it by just emphasis.

The air *But Thou Didst Not Leave His Soul in Hell* moves a shade too fast and is sung without the necessary repose. Diction and tone are excellent and so is the recording A.R.

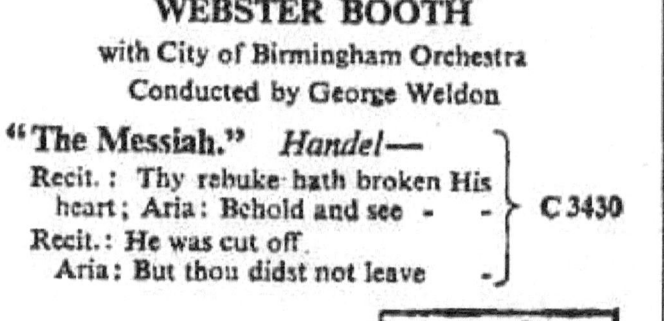

WEBSTER BOOTH

with City of Birmingham Orchestra
Conducted by George Weldon

"The Messiah." *Handel—*

Recit. : Thy rebuke hath broken His
heart ; Aria : Behold and see - - } C 3430
Recit.: He was cut off.
Aria : But thou didst not leave -

July 1945
War records
Other labels bear the names of Webster Booth, Sydney Burchall and Clarence Wright, who take part in **Songs Our Boys Sang** and **Marching Times**.

These records are not for sale to the general public, but sets are available at most of the 5300 National Savings Centres throughout the Country. Further information will gladly be given by the National Savings Committee, Sanctuary Buildings, Great Smith Street, SW1.

November 1945

Anne Ziegler (soprano), **Webster Booth** (tenor), with orchestra.
Liebestraüm (Dowdon-Liszt, arr. Besly) : **Nocturne** (Dowdon-Chopin, arr. Besty). H.M.V. C3460 (12 in., 6s. 7d.)

A few more records like this and the sweet ration will become unnecessary. It is difficult to be consistent about arrangements. Liszt, of course, wrote his Liebestraurne as solo songs and that might be considered, by some, as sufficient justification for making duets out of them. No such justification can be found for snaking a duet out of Chopin's Nocturne in B flat: but if it is played in arrangements for violin, cello, and perhaps the ocarina, I suppose a vocal duet can come into the picture as well. The singing and recording are good: and if you like this sort of thing it is the sort of thing you will like.

April 1946
Webster Booth (tenor) Gerald Moore (piano): *There is no Death* (Johnson/O'Hara): *Just for Today* (Partridge/Seaver) HMV B9458
I particularly dislike the type of religiosity represented in these songs but there is no doubt that it makes a wide appeal, and so I will only say that the songs are very well sung by Webster Booth, every word can be heard and the recording is good.

July 1946

Anne Zeigler and Webster Booth have made a recording for which, I am sure, a great many people have been waiting—their version of We'll gather lilacs from "Perchance to Dream." I am sure that the majority of people will already have heard them sing this delightful number on the radio and therefore any comment of mine would be superfluous. The coupling is the now well-known and popular Love steals your heart which was featured in the film "The Wicked Lady." As always their singing and diction is delightful (H.M.V. B9489).

August 1946

Anne Ziegler and Webster Booth sing two delightful numbers from the film **The Laughing Lady.** *Laugh at Life* is sung in fast waltz tempo and reminds me very much of some of the charming tunes which have been written around films of life in Vienna when it was the gayest of capitals. *Love is the Key*, on the other side, is, if anything, the better of the two, and here again one is impressed by the unforced gaiety and excellence of the singing of these famous artists (HMV B9490) H. S.

September 1946

Whenever I hear Webster Booth singing lieder I regret that he should not, from the start, have devoted his talents to the concert hall instead of giving himself up to light music and only occasionally singing music of more serious character. His performance of Grieg's *Ich Liebe Dich*, in a poor translation, is free from over-emphasis and he uses the resources of a voice of beautiful quality, but not much power, so skillfully as to produce the necessary climax at the fourth repetition of the amatory phrase.

Schumann's *Widmung* lacks the exalted fervour it must have and the singer does not make nearly enough of the middle section, deceptively quiet but actually tense and always ready to burst, as it does, into the passion of the opening tune. Gerald Moore's accompaniments are as admirable as ever. He supports the voice, in the Grieg, with just the right amount of tone in the left-hand part, where it doubles the voice part, and his exact observance of the characteristic dotted note in the first section of *Widmung* should be a lesson to budding accompanists. The balance between voice and piano is fairly good.

October 1946
Webster Booth (tenor), Gerald Moore (piano): *All Soul's Day*, opus No 8 (Bernhoff/Richard Strauss); *Memory Island* (Askew/Harrison) HMV B9502 (10")

Richard Strauss's setting of *All Soul's Day* calls for singing of considerable emotional stress, and when Webster Booth gets impassioned his voice loses the easy charm that is its chief characteristic. His words are a model of distinctness and the accompaniment of Gerald Moore is perfect, but the song is not a very happy choice.

The singer is more at home in *Memory Island*, in which a sailor home from the sea for good, casts his memory back, Masefield-wise, to the blue lagoons, coral islands and what not of the rover. It is a nice song with, for its type, an unusually good accompaniment.

November 1946
This foretaste of Christmas is also to be found in a record by Webster Booth, who graces this column with a visit. Gounod's *Nazareth* and *O Come all Ye Faithful*, both with organ accompaniment, will make a nice present for lots of nice people, but surely the essence of hymn singing is congregational, and one misses the great burst of sound that should mark the last verse of this hymn, though Booth does his best, reminding us of Heinrich Schlusnuss coming round for the last verse of Schubert's *Who is Sylvia?* (HMV B9507)

January 1947
Webster Booth breaks new ground in a riotous drinking song from his new film **Laughing Lady**. The music is by Hans May. The *Wine Song* (destined to be another *Stein Song*) starts with a rough and tumble by the chorus before Mr Booth raises his melodious tenor above the din and takes charge of the proceedings. On the other side Anne Ziegler

sings, very charmingly, *I'll Change My Heart*, one of her numbers from the film. (HMV B9518)

March 1947
A Perfect Day/Always
And Webster Booth has made a record both intrinsically attractive and timely. Carrie Jacobs Bond died earlier this year in America after a heroic life, which in The Times obituary reads like an old romance – which is indeed what it was. She it was who wrote **A Perfect Day**, and it is by this that she will live in the hearts of simple people who are not too proud to cherish a simple song. This is backed by the *other* **Always**, which Kenneth Leslie-Smith wrote for the broadcast musical show, **Puritan Lullaby**. It is a long time since ma Souez did this, and Mr Booth has seldom given us so attractive a coupling in the popular field (HMV B9534).

May 1947
(Stanford Robinson): *Total Eclipse*, **Samson** (Handel); *In Native Worth*, **The Creation** (Haydn). HMV C3571 (12")
Both these songs are associated with the last days of their respective composers. When Handel was old and blind, the London public enjoyed nothing so much as to watch him at the keyboard and to shed comfortable tears while the great John Beard sang *Total Eclipse*. As Haydn lay dying, a French officer representing the invaders of Haydn's country visited the composer and sang to him *In Native Worth*. This then is a record with an almost overwhelming historical and sentimental appeal.

The Handel is probably a first recording; certainly no other is listed in current English catalogues. What character Handel breathed into the rigid formalism of contemporary music! See how the despair of the little introductory symphony to the aria is immediately lightened before the voice begins. The song itself is of ineffable beauty, and once again, Webster Booth shows he is of the stature to sing this music. It is earnestly to be hoped that he will go on recording Handel. The greatest writer for the human voice happened to write his finest work in English, and it is not every generation that can produce the singers for it. We still await a bass to succeed McEachern. It is interesting to recall that the text of **The Creation** was prepared before Handel's death and was presumably intended for him. For Haydn, who called Handel "the master of us all," it was a fortuitous challenge in the history of music. Listening to this record one thinks back to Handel and forward to Schubert; both are there and these reflections show once again the strength and width of the great bridge that was Joseph Haydn. Every word crystal clear, every phrase a musician's dream and the finest Abbey Road recording. In short a record to be enjoyed over the years, which is what records are for. R.W.

June 1947
Webster Booth is joined by Anne Ziegler in two duets on HMV B9552. Landon Ronald's *O Lovely Night* would have been better sung by one or the other, but a revival of *Dearest Love* from Noel Coward's **Operette** comes off well enough.

July 1947
What a singer is Webster Booth. I know there are some who will say he is colourless and always the well-groomed salon tenor whether he is singing Handel or Madame d'Hardelot. He certainly takes kindly to the gramophone, and this month scores an obvious winner with Sanderson's *Until* and Teresa del Riego's *O Dry Those Tears*. I have a very warm corner for the best of the Edwardian ballads, which are so well laid out for the voice apart from being spanking good tunes and Mr Booth gives these all he has got without even a hint of distortion. Who will ever forget D'Alvarez's record of Madame Del Riego's *Homing*? This song may not be in the

same class, but it is of the same genre, and most welcome, I'm sure. (HMV B9562).

October 1947
Webster Booth is I suppose rather naughty to have sung words to **Greensleeves**. I do not know whose words they are, for the perpetrator hides under initials, while the tune is arranged by Olive Richardson. There is really nothing to give offence, and I am sure the Elizabethans would have been delighted, while Easthope Martin cannot but be charmed by Mr Booth's singing of his **Everywhere I Go**, one of the **Four Pastorales**, on HMV B9585.

February 1948
Here are some records on the border line of "Miscellaneous" and Operatic and Songs from singers who so adroitly find themselves in either category. Webster Booth has a real winner in two popular ballads—Stephen Adams' **Nirvana** and Tosti's **My Dreams**, both with words by the indefatigable Fred Weatherley, and both supremely well sung. Accompaniments are on the heavy side, especially at climaxes, where it is so easy for everybody to let go, when it is just there that it is so important to hold the reins.
(HMV B9617).

March 1948
At the opposite extreme as a safe bet for everybody is the duet arrangements of two well-loved songs sung by Anne Ziegler and Webster Booth on HMV B9627. Mendelssohn's **On Wings of Song** is the second of the six making up Op. 34. The numerous existing recordings were listed in December by Lionel Salter, but there is always room for one more. Carl Bohm's **Still as the Night** is on the reverse. He and Brahms shared the same publisher, and it is said that the popularity of the former paid for the latter, which gives him a special place in musical history. Both arrangements

are by Doris Arnold, and the blend of voices is nicely tuned. There is an orchestra conducted by Eric Robinson.

April 1948
Mr Booth chooses Tauber's song *My Heart and I* from **Old Chelsea**, and if you can bear to hear anyone else sing this there is probably no one better. Reverse carries *Break of Day* by Hans May, composer of the music for **Carissima** (B 9633).

June 1948
Webster Booth (tenor) with orchestra, conducted by George Melachrino: *Napoli Bay* (Kynoch); *Show Me the Way* (O'Connor/Morgan). HMV B9640 (10" 4/8)
    A record for this singer's most devoted admirers. The songs are unexceptionable and call for no comment.

October 1948
Webster Booth (tenor) Orchestra conducted by Braithwaite. *Love in Her Eyes Sits Playing* and *Love Sounds the Alarm*, from **Acis and Galatea** (Handel) HMV C3796 (12", 5/9)
What a fine tenor we have in Mr Webster Booth! *Love Sounds the Alarm* is sung with a virility and rhythm which I find most invigorating. Every word is as clear as day too. The orchestral playing (and the recording) is excellent and this is altogether a most satisfying side. On the reverse I feel we could have had more lightness: the performance is rather exhausting to listen to. After hearing both sides one feels that it is all very loud and I am sure that *Love in Her Eyes* would gain by far lighter treatment from the orchestra as well as from the singer.
    Indeed, the orchestra on this side is a little too loud even for the singing (which Mr Booth maintains at a good forte). But if you do not play both sides successively you will enjoy them very much. The recording is bright and lively.

December 1948
*Mr Webster Booth singing operetta is as sympathetic to my ear as can be. His voice is grateful to listen to and his style has real charm. A warm and sympathetic recording too.
*There is no mention in the magazine of the titles on this recording! I have looked through my own discography and think that the recording discussed is: B9703 **Wayside rose/Frederica;Serenade/Frasquita**/Léhar,December 1948

April 1949
HMV C3844, **The Long Day Closes** (Sullivan) and **God be in My Head** (Walford Davies). These lovely works are sung by the Tommy Handley Memorial Choir under Leslie Woodgate, unaccompanied; the choir includes such famous names as Norman Allin, Webster Booth, Parry Jones and Dennis Noble, and as the last notes of the second side die away, Charles Smart at the organ plays Walford Davies **Solemn melody** to round off a delightful record, whereon the diction is perfect and the execution everything that anyone could desire. Profits from the sales are to go to the National Association of Girls' Clubs and Mixed Clubs, and the National Association of Boys' Clubs, jointly.

March 1949
Webster Booth and Anne Ziegler sing two very suitable songs – **Hear My Song, Violetta** and **Love's Last Word is Spoken** on HMV B9738, though, I think, Anne Ziegler could be a little clearer.

June 1949
Webster Booth (tenor), with orchestra, cond. George Melachrino: **'Tis the Day** (Leoncavallo): **If You are There** (Ege-North). HMV B9777 (10", 4s. 8d.).
    Mr Webster Booth sings these two ballads with his usual good voice and admirable diction. He suggests the Italian style in Leoncavallo's song but wisely sings Michael

Head's* little piece in simpler manner. The orchestra is the sort that is too often got together to accompany ballads, the assumption being, I suppose, that people who enjoy these songs do not listen to what goes on behind the voice. Here the violins are thin and stringy—notice their unpleasant start in *If You are There*. On the reverse they have less to do and the result is happier. The recording is adequate.

The pleasure this disc will give, however, will undoubtedly come from Mr Booth's singing. Since writing the above, a letter has arrived from an American reader pointing out that our reviewers of vocal records misuse the word "diction." Diction, he says—and correctly—means choice of words or phraseology. Therefore it cannot ever be used of singers who never choose their words. But it is so generally used by musicians to suggest not only clarity of words but also the artist's sensitivity to their colour that I think it is high time the dictionaries admitted this use. Many other common, if incorrect, usages have become so general that dictionaries have had to accept them. A language, after all, is a living thing and many of its children cannot claim the purest parentage. I am grateful for Mr McGraw's reminder but unrepentant! T.H.

If You are There is not by Michael Head, but by Michael North!

August 1949

I entirely agree with A. R. Morris who suggested, in the May edition of THE GRAMOPHONE, that there should be more of the popular operas recorded in English.

The only "popular" opera that remains in the catalogues (Australian and English), sung in English, is Columbia's **Faust**; surely the fact that it has remained in the catalogue for so many years would be enough to prompt one of the recording companies to bring out other operas sung in English. There is a wealth of talented singers in England at present, such as Webster Booth, Joan Hammond, Dennis

Noble, Heddle Nash, Gwen Catley, to name a few, who should be capable of helping to produce most excellent sets.

I hope the companies will consider that there is a reasonable market for opera in English and, if I may say so, I think it would be an excellent opportunity for Decca to build up their Catalogue of F.F.R.R. Opera.

Sydney, N.S.W. **W. A. SALTER**.

December 1949

HANDEL. Recit.: My **arms! against this Gorgias will I** go. Aria: **Sound an Alarm** from "Judas Maccabaeus." Why **dees the God of Israel sleep** from "Samson" **Webster Booth** (tenor), with orch. cond. Braithwaite. H.M.V. C3939 12 in,, 5s. gd.

How admirably Mr. Webster Booth sings Handel! To these excellent performances on his part is added vivid orchestral playing,the whole very well recorded. As to the singing, the voice is of fine timbre, the vocal technique first-rate, the words as clear as can be, and every phrase is sung with real conviction. Let the many amateur tenors who sing Sound an Alarm at Competition Festivals take this as a model. T.H.

1/3 NINETEEN-FIFTIES - NINETEEN SIXTIES

February 1950

Vocal

Considering the more "serious" singers first, we find **Anne Ziegler** and **Webster Booth** pouring out some mellow old-world music from Messager's operetta "Veronique" on H.M.V. B9870 (*Swing High, Swing Low* and *Trot Here, Trot There*). **Gracie Fields** contributes a rather prefabricated pastorale in *The Shepherd*, and the famous *Song of the Mountains* from "The Glass Mountain" (Decca F9312), while **Jane Powell**, the new American singing star of the film "Nancy Goes to Rio," sings two items from that film, *Love is Like This* and (in Italian) Musetta's waltz song, *Quando m'en vo'* from "La Bohème" (M.G.M. 260). I wish M.G.M. would learn how to balance and record soprani ; this is very squeaky, and I will adhere firmly to Ljuba Welitsch's Musetta rather than have this version.

December 1950
There is some straightforward tenor music by Webster Booth on HMV B9999 *Where Haven Lies* from Edward German's **The Princess of Kensington** is Booth's métier completely, but his voice does not seem robust enough for Sullivan's *Drinking Song* from **The Rose of Persia**.

March 1951
Turning to the more acceptable artists, we find Webster Booth singing *No More* and *May the Good Lord Bless and Keep You* on HMV B10035. This will delight his many fans.

July 1951
Webster Booth is quite ordinary and competent on HMV B10092 in *Where E'r You Go* and a semi-religious song, *At*

the End of the Day, which is rather redolent of Christopher Robin.

August 1952
On the Decca label Webster Booth (F9942) sings *The White Dove* typically, and to the tune of Lincke's *Luna Waltz*, *Castles in the Air*, pronouncing the first word "cassels" and giving the accompanying orchestra a generous share of the work.

November 1957
NIGHTS AT THE ROUND TABLE by W. A. CHISLETT
I have such a jorum (if ! may be pardoned a North-country quantitative noun) of EPs that I had better start there this month and what better to begin with than a few reissues of old favourites.

Webster Booth and Joan Cross were among the best of English operatic singers during the same years and they usually sang in English. In **Operatic Favourites**, No. I they sing *Lovely Maid in the Moonlight* from **La Bohème**, the *Miserere* from **Il Trovatore**, *When Stars were Brightly Shining* from **Tosca** and Webster Booth is joined by Noel Eadie, Edith Coates and Arnold Matters in the quartet from **Rigoletto**. An excellent and eminently desirable dubbing.

OPERAGOERS often complain that British singers cannot be heard on record. Before the war one could buy records of Joan Cross, Webster Booth, and Dennis Noble (some of them survive in LP format), but the gramophone companies have not taken the appeal of Sadler's Wells (and, since 1946, Covent Garden) favourites as a standard part of recording policy; since the arrival of LP Joan Hammond has been the sole stay of British opera on records.

October 1959

July 1964
Ziegler and Booth
On opening THE GRAMOPHONE this month I was delighted to see, on page 6, under the heading "Index to Reviews—Collections" the entry "Duets—Ziegler and Booth page 29". However, much to my dismay on turning up page 29, I had to note that only a 45 rpm single had been issued of these most charming artists, and even this of two rather hackneyed arias *Indian Love Call* from **Rose Marie** and *Barcarolle* from **Tales of Hoffmann**, though their renditions of even these are most delightful. Being in possession of ten of their old 78s and deriving such great pleasure from every one of them, I am astonished that EMI have never apparently thought of issuing at least a 10-inch LP of some of these fine old discs by Webster Booth and Anne Ziegler, who surely were so popular.
Brussels, Belgium. **W. E. BROWN**.

January 1966
Anne Ziegler and Webster Booth were one of the most popular of husband and wife teams. They both had successful individual careers in the 1930s before their marriage. Possibly their first appearance together (and this was before their marriage) was in the first English colour film, Faust, in which they sang Margaret and Faust respectively. It was about the beginning of the second world war that they began their double act and toured together, singing romantic duets from musicals, in towns throughout Britain and in the Commonwealth. Many will recall them in the successful 1943 revival of The Vagabond King in which they took over the roles originally created by Derek Oldham and Winnie Melville in 1927. They made countless records together and this selection is typical of them. Both have voices and musical sensibilities far above the average of those who sing in musical comedy and they are voices that are not only good individually but which blend unusually well. I do not know the dates of the original recordings but whatever these may be the sound here is both fresh and immediate.

1/4
NINETEEN-SEVENTIES TO PRESENT DAY

OCTOBER 1970
LOOKING BACK—OCTOBER 1929
I was visited this summer by Mr George Lepan, a reader in Toronto, who kindly brought all the way from Canada two precious records issued by American Columbia in memory of Gershwin with Carroll Gibbons as anchor pianist. Since these records are compèred by Christopher Stone, for years London Editor of THE GRAMOPHONE, who refers topically to the composer's death, these must date from about 1937. Does any reader know if they were ever issued here They must have been made here, for no American would be likely to choose Anne Ziegler and Webster Booth to sing extracts from **Porgy and Bess**, which they sing extremely well. Others taking part are Larry Adler and Hildegarde, with extracts from the Astaire **Lady be Good** records, cleverly interpolated, Gibbons taking over from the composer's piano dead in tune. A most moving gift from overseas. My senior colleagues would blush if they could hear Mr Lepan's views on their reviews, but it is always heartening to know one is read so far away. [The Adler/Hildegarde/Astaire record was made in London as a tribute to Gershwin one afternoon just prior to the August Bank Holiday of 1937, some 3 weeks after Gershwin's death. It was issued the same month as Columbia DX786. The Ziegler/Booth record followed in February 1938 as DX824. Ed.]

March 1971
British tenors
I would like to make a plea to EMI which has been prompted by my purchase of the recent release **Famous British Tenors** (HMV mono HQM1228-9/70). May we have some further releases as soon as possible? As one of the younger generation I sat spellbound through most of the recordings.

It's amazing to think that our land has produced voices of such rare beauty (and that, only in the tenor category!). Yet it is shocking that our catalogues are virtually devoid of further recordings by most of these artists.

Two names which are today virtually forgotten or indeed depending upon your age unheard of, are Parry Jones and Webster Booth. Please EMI, let us have these names featured in your *Golden Voice* Series—they are worthy of it. It is a sad state of affairs when we are forced to state that our only chance of listening to voices such as these is on old, cracking, badly worn 78s.

Finally, what of Walter Midgley? His recordings are much fresher and clearer than many of his colleagues featured in the above mentioned recording. Such a voice is worthy of a place in our catalogues. It is not enough to issue an LP providing only a taste of the artist's talent. What a wonderful heritage we have, if only it was more readily available.

"Please sir, I want some more!"
Aberdeen. **Alistair MeRorsa**.

September 1972

COLLECTORS' CORNER by BRIAN RUST

Light Opera Companies
The inexhaustible topic of pseudonyms continues to absorb our readers' interest, and Mr J. W. Watson (Hull) wonders who were the singers who contributed so ably to the HMV and Columbia "Light Opera Companies" that made hosts of records of "vocal gems" from current musical comedies, operas, operettas and past musical productions. Alas, there doesn't seem to be anything left now that will identify them beyond question, but I do know that HMV used such well-known singers as Bessie Jones, Violet Essex, George Baker, Ernest Pike, Edward Halland, Nellie Walker and

Eleanor Jones-Hudson (yes, the same one as I mentioned in connection with the Alvena Yarrow mystery) during the first world war years and after; it is also a fact that the soloist in **The Blue Mazurka** selection on HMV was the star of the show, Elizabeth Pechy. During the earlier thirties, Webster Booth, Stuart Robertson, Suzanne Botterill, Foster Richardson and Olive Groves were often employed, I believe. Victor had a comparably static roster of fine singers, which included during the years 1913-1929 an outstanding singer who could and did cope with everything from sacred music to Broadway hits via opera and concert music: the glorious soprano Olive Kline, at this writing still living and in good health, in New York. Her colleagues included at different times such great artists as Richard Crooks, Reinald Werrenrath, Lambert Murphy, Elsie Baker and, on the more permanently lighter side, Billy Murray, the 'cute' sounding Belle Mann, and sometimes Frank Crummit.

November 1973
Webster Booth reissue
I would like to make a plea for the reissue of some of the 78 rpm discs made by Webster Booth. Although he was known in personal appearances primarily as a singer of ballads and musical comedy, his recordings covered oratorio and opera. Indeed during the thirties and forties he probably made more records than any other British singer.

He was served by consistently good recordings and in a wide range of material maintained an extraordinarily high standard of performance.

I have always thought it poor criticism to praise one artist at the expense of another, yet I have found it incomprehensible that the recordings of Booth's contemporary, Heddle Nash should have been lauded, without so much as a mention of Webster Booth's versions. Where comparisons are possible, I cannot call to mind a single instance of Nash producing a superior version. In support of my contention I would cite arias from **Messiah, Judas Maccabeus, Jephtha, Don Giovanni, Magic Flute Carmen, Faust, Bohème** and lighter fare.

I do not doubt that Heddle Nash enjoyed a superior reputation as an opera singer and in the concert hall. He was moreover an artist who was able to project much charm in his personal appearances. I wonder if this has caused critics and the public to over-rate his recordings to the detriment of those of Webster Booth.

DONALD HUDSON, West Ardsley, Yorkshire.

14 March 2009 20:04   Report this comment

While Webster Booth is remembered today primarily for his appearances on the Variety stage with his wife, Anne Ziegler, he not only made many oratorio recordings as Mr Hudson pointed out, but he was one of the foremost oratorio soloists of his generation. He found time to appear regularly on the concert platform in a variety of oratorios and considered his work in that field to have been the most rewarding. He was a notable Gerontius in Elgar's "Dream of Gerontius" and appeared in many presentations of "Hiawatha's Wedding Feast".

I have been interested to read the Gramophone archive with reference to Webster Booth and to see how often critics at the time considered his voice to be one of the finest in Britain and hoped that he would devote himself regularly to more serious work.

Jean Collen, Johannesburg

December 1973
Webster Booth
I support the letter from Mr Donald Hudson (November, p. 915) regarding a reissue of some of the recordings made by Webster Booth, for one only has to check the last HMV 78rpm catalogue to realise that this artist's records were selling well until the demise of 78s. I cannot understand how it is that we have had several LPs of Heddle Nash, Richard Tauber, Peter Dawson and quite a few others, but never a solo LP by Webster Booth. If an LP should arrive might I put in a plea for one special item, the beautiful *Love Duet* from **Madame Butterfly** with Joan Hammond HMV C3376) with the Liverpool Philharmonic Orchestra conducted by Sargent, and of course I hope there would be more of the wonderful

opera arias that this great artist recorded. Portslade, Sussex.
WILLIAM C GUMBELL

I should like to heartily endorse Mr Hudson's comments on the high quality of the performances of Webster Booth and join in his plea for an LP reissue of his bet recordings.

Like Mr Hudson I, too, find Booth's recordings of particular songs or arias superior in most cases to those of Nash. The latter's Italian training gave him a better line and in the flesh he probably had the larger voice, but Booth never suffered from the whiteness of tone which afflicted Nash (on record at least) and he was able to take in full voice high C's which forced Nash into near falsetto.

Booth certainly did not have a great voice (neither did Schipa!) and his tone lacked much of the sweetness and clarity of these fine but also neglected tenors, Walter Glynne and Walter Midgley. So in what did Booth's attraction lie?

I find his recordings pleasing because he was able to bring a spontaneous quality to his interpretations which were enhanced by his ability and willingness to colour his light voice in a most remarkable way (a point which might usefully be noted by so many of today's efficient but monotonous singers).

Examples of this variety abound. The dignity of his *Total Eclipse* from Handel's **Samson**, is enhanced by the almost baritonal breadth of tone. By contrast, the slight material of *Macushla* and *I'll Walk beside You* is transformed by that magical high mezza-voce into something greater. The vivid declamation of *Heavenly Aida* leads to a truly dolce final B flat, the only one I know on record. The inward anguish of the *Flower Song* from Bizet's **Carmen** is, for once, brought out by gentle singing and *Your Tiny Hand* from Puccini's **La Bohème** (in my opinion) is one of the finest ever recorded.

So, please, let us have a reissue of his best recordings of opera, oratorio and ballads. **DH CLAMPTON**, Barrow-in-Furness, Lancs

April 1974
Webster Booth
Letters in the November (p 915) and December (p 1186) issues concerning Webster Booth encourage me to write and tell those who admire this tenor of his present whereabouts.

In 1951 (*sic*) he and Anne Ziegler, his wife and partner, decided to live in South Africa, a country of which they had retained happy memories from their concert work just after the last war. For eleven years they ran a voice studio in Johannesburg until the early nineteen-sixties (sic) they bought a home three hundred miles from Cape Town at Paradise on the banks of the Knysna Lagoon. Webster Booth, who is now 72 years old, conducts the local choral society of which Anne is the producer. A few pupils keep them occupied happily as they stage such old favourites as **Messiah, Elijah, The Crucifixion, Merrie England** and an annual Christmas pantomime.

In a letter from him a good while ago now, Mr Booth told me of his great admiration for Harold Williams whom he holds as an example for oratorio pupils. "He was a wonderful singer who taught me a lot".

I had hoped to include an article on this popular tenor in **Singers to Remember** but could not assemble my material in time. Although I hold his oratorio recordings in higher esteem than his operatic ones there are many who will disagree with me. Rococo reissued a poor selection and EMI could certainly do greater justice to this favourite artist. Indeed he is but one of several British singers crying out for representation on LP: Norman Allin, Muriel Brunskill, Miriam Licette to name but three...

Harold Simpson, Gladstone, Queensland, Australia

May 1977
Webster Booth LP
The appeal of voices is so much a matter of personal taste that my failure to capitulate wholly, as others do (*pace* some recent correspondence in these columns), to Webster Booth's attractive singing may to some extent be blamed on the way I hear his voice. That he was innately musical, enunciated with admirable clarity, and always paid attention to the appropriate style of the piece he was interpreting is confirmed by this far-ranging recital. At the same time it confirms his limitations. There is a bland sameness about all his singing, a lack of those individual accents that make an interpretation memorable, and a continual lack of variety in his predominantly pleasing timbre.

For none of these items, except perhaps for the *Faery Song* would I turn to Booth for a preferred performance. Nash is so much more eloquent in Handel and as *Faust* (listen to his legato at the start and to Booth's comparative lack of it), to David Lloyd for the Ottavio in **Don Giovanni** arias, to Widdop for the **Elijah**, to Tudor Davies for *Onaway! Awake beloved*, to Hislop for *The English Rose*. In each case their phrases lodge themselves in the mind, and make you want to hear their interpretations again and again.

Without those withering comparisons, Booth has, as I say, much to offer in sheer professionalism and good taste. How few Italian tenors will end *Celeste Aida* (here given in a horrible translation) with a piano high B flat. Indeed how many of them would be capable of doing so? How many French ones would do the same at the end of the *Flower Song*? Yet one cannot believe that Booth would have had the wherewithal to tackle either Radames or José on stage, although he could deliver quite hearty top C's, as you can hear in the **Faust** and **Bohème** arias.

The choice of items has on the whole been sensible, except that I would have included his moving *Total eclipse*, the **Entführung** aria, and the delightful **Barber** duet with

Dennis Noble. That and the close of **Bohème** Act 1 with Joan Cross might have broken a certain air of monotony.

The recordings, mostly made in Liverpool (the three with the Hallé made in the Holdsworth Hall in Manchester, show a startling improvement in sound), are reliable, the transfers first-rate. Now can we have LPs of Noble, Tudor Davies and Hislop please. A B

June 1980
SONG RECITAL. Stuart Burrows (tenor), John Constable (piano). L'Oiseau-Lyre DSL043 (E5.25); C)KDSLC43 (£5.25).
This record follows a similar collection which was reviewed by JBS (April, page 1596) and I am delighted to learn that there is a third to follow. As with JBS, Stuart Burrows often recalls Webster Booth to me, and that is a commendation indeed, especially in this sort of music which is so seemingly simple but far from easy to put across successfully. An admirable addition to the now numerous revivals of songs with so many of which I was very familiar in my boyhood and youth. Among those which I am most glad to hear again are *I Heard You Singing, Sitting by the Window* and *In the Gloaming*. As always John Constable is an ideal accompanist. W.A.C.

June 1982
But for light music from the archives there is one clear recommendation, also from World Records, the latest in their superlative series of Gilbert and Sullivan reissues. The unequalled 1930 recording of **Patience** is coupled on SHB74 (mono 2 records) with that abridged version of **The Gondoliers** which appeared originally in depression-stricken 1931 on the cheap plum label, and one fancies that the exceptional verve of the performance may owe something to the challenge of fitting the items on to the ten-inch discs. The smaller parts are strongly cast, with names like Essie

Ackland, Webster Booth and Stuart Robertson; there is George Baker's quick-fire Duke of Plaza-Toro; and in *There Lived a King* Sydney Granville can be heard giving what one would have said if dates permitted was a masterly impersonation of Dennis Healey. The **Patience** has Baker, Fancourt, Oldham, the magnificent Bertha Lewis, and Winifred Lawson exquisite in her *Love is a Plaintive Song*. Sargent's touch was never surer, and Keith Hardwick's transfers are a model of what such things should be. Joy unbounded. J.B.S.

September 1984

The singer Webster Booth has also died, at 82, in Llandudno. Renowned for the duo with his wife, Anne Ziegler, he began his adult life studying accountancy, but soon began appearing with the D'Oyly Carte Company (*Yeomen of the Guard*, 1924) with whom he toured. Booth's—and the duo's—repertoire offered a much-needed, if sentimental, diversion from the depression of the Second World War, during which he and Anne Ziegler were familiar voices on the radio in such songs as *We'll gather lilacs* and *The Lord's Prayer*.

April 1996

Stars of English Opera

December 19th Lovely morning with Dennis Noble! And last night many furtive tears over the once despised plum labels – Catley, Booth *et al*. And Dutton do it again!

Ah, the internecine strife, the near-ends to beautiful friendships, in days of old! The few of us who were interested in operatic records during school-days in wartime were a close band of brothers till it came to the burning issue: plum-label opera in English versus red-label Italian (or very occasionally, German, French or Russian). Against my Marcella Sembrich they would range their puny Gwen Catley, and my mighty Martinelli their skinny Webster Booth. But now the old battle-cries rally no troops, and all I find is that a pleasure deferred is a pleasure enhanced.

Stars of English Opera (Dutton Laboratories CDLX7018) has Catley's Dearest name (**Rigoletto**), close-miked but faultlessly clean and well-schooled. Booth contributes *O Vision Entrancing* (**Esmeralda**), and he's not Tom Burke: never mind, clean-cut and well-mannered. Janet Howe, Gladys Ripley, John Hargreaves, Redvers Llewellyn: names once so familiar and their memories well served in these solos. Outstanding among them all, Oscar Natzke is in magnificent form as Falstaff in **The Merry Wives of Windsor**. And Dennis Noble's Rossini **Figaro**, a fellow of infinite resource, is a great delight, as is the disc devoted to him also on Dutton (CDLX7017) reviewed by myself in this present issue. The star of stars, it must be said is the Dutton Labs and their transfer-work: clear and bright but mercifully free of the harshness and aggressive "top" that disfigures so many.

October 2005
Singing Styles
I was interested to read John Steane's article about changing styles in singing (July, page 49). There is no doubt that the old acoustic recordings are off-putting to some people, as is the stylised singing of tenors such as Webster Booth and Heddle Nash which mirrors the *portamento* violin style in orchestras of the time...

Mannered singing by "classical" voices may well be dying out but it is still very much a feature of popular music and as a result likely soon to sound dated.
THOMAS E ROCKERS, Lincoln, Lincs

I don't think so: indeed, when I was attempting to make a career as a tenor during the 1980s it was Widdop I most wished to sound like (needless to say, I didn't!). I could say much in praise of Heddle Nash and Webster Booth also; might John Steane consider British pre-war tenors at some future date?
PAUL WILSON
SOUTH CROYDON, SURREY, UK

PART TWO - DISCOGRAPHY

2/1 RECORDS ON LABELS OTHER THAN HMV

Brunswick/Rex

+**SA1573A/B** Sweethearts; Wooden Shoes/**Sweethearts/** Herbert, Carlo Santana (Harry Bidgood) accordion orchestra,

+**SA1588-A/B** One Day When We Were Young; Tales from the Vienna Woods/**The Great Waltz**/Strauss, Unnamed soprano, Carlo Santana (Harry Bidgood) accordion orchestra

+**Rex 9201** Giannina Mia; Sympathy/ **Firefly**/Friml, Carlo Santana (Harry Bidgood) accordion orchestra, 1938

Columbia

DX691 West End Nights: **Gay Deceivers**: You are me, Serenade; **Stop Press**! You and the Night and the Music; **Easter Parade**, with Webster Booth, Muriel Barron, Marjorie Stedeford, chorus, Debroy Somers, 16 May 1935/ July 1935

*****DX824 Porgy and Bess Selection**/Gershwin/Carroll Gibbons/10 January 1938

DX832 Snow White and the Seven Dwarfs Medley/Morey with Nora Savage, Webster Booth, Orchestra of Merry Men, directed by George Scott-Wood and vocal quartet Side 1: I'm Wishing, One Song, With a Smile and a Song. Side 2: Whistle While You Work, Heigh-ho, Dwarfs' Yodel Song, Some Day My Prince Will Come, 1938

Decca

Decca K628 Rosemarie Vocal Selection/Friml/ Victor Conway, Anne Welch, Webster Booth, 12 December 1930

Decca K644 Goodnight Vienna Vocal Selection/George Posford/Webster Booth with Olive Groves, May 1932

*Decca F 9887 Love Calling Me Home/We'll Find A Way, Harry Parr Davies, April 1952

Decca F 9910 Star of Hope/Phil Boutelje/Harry Tobias/ Emile Waldteufel; Give and Forgive/D. O'Keefe, May 1952

Decca F9921 Sanctuary of the Heart/Ketelby; He Bought My Heart At Calvary/Hamblen with choir of St Stephen's Church Dulwich, Fela Sowande (organ) June 1952

Decca F9942 Castles in the Air/Lincke; The White Dove/Léhar, July 1952

Durium

M-41171-A What More Can I Ask?; Brighter Than the Sun/ from film *The Little Damozel*, Durium Dance Orchestra, Peter Rush,1 February 1933

M-41172 Speak to Me of Love/Lenoir/Sievier; Tell Me Tonight/Mischa Spoliansky, Durium Dance Orchestra, Peter Rush, December 1932/1 February 1933

Regal-Zonophone

G22075 A Brown Bird Singing/Wood; A Little Love, a Little Kiss/Lao Silesu/Fred Hartley's Quintet, CAR 2468

(Australian pressing)1934

MR1220 Roses of Picardy/Wood; Bird Songs at Eventide, Coates/Fred Hartley's Quintet, CAR2467/9 March 1934

MR1228 Serenade/Toselli; In Old Madrid/Trotiere, Fred Hartley's Quintet, June 1934

2/2 HMV – B RECORDINGS (10")

Test recording Serenata, Macushla Reginald Paul, C Studio, Small Queens Hall, London, 20 November 1929

B3283 Dance Away the Night/**Married In Hollywood/** Dave Stamper and Harlam Thompson; Let Me Dream in Your Arms Again/Nicholls, Ray Noble/New Mayfair Orchestra, Kingsway Hall, London, 18 December 1929,1932

B3319 I Love the Moon/Rubens; A Brown Bird Singing/Wood, Ray Noble/New Mayfair Orchestra/ with nightingale song, Kingsway Hall, London, 18 December 1929, May 1930

B3448 Patriotic Medley; Princess Elizabeth/Crean/Patience Strong, Richard Crean, London Palladium Orchestra, Studio C, Small Queens Hall, 20 May 1930,Bb19321

B3735 Somewhere a Voice is Calling/Tate; I Know of Two Bright Eyes/Clutsam, Ray Noble, New Mayfair Orchestra, Friends Meeting House, London,10 January 1930/April 1931

B3758 Moonlight and You/De Crescenzo; Always as I Close My Eyes/ Coates,Ray Noble,New Mayfair Orchestra, Studio C, Small Queens Hall, London, 30 December 1930/1931 Bb21105/6

B3778 Heavenly Night /Brown; Along the Road of Dreams/Granichstaedten/ **One Heavenly Night/**Ray Noble, New Mayfair Orchestra, 2 February 1931, OB355/6-2

B3866-71The Gondoliers/Gilbert & Sullivan/Abridged Sargent, Webster Booth as Luiz, 1931

B8385 Heart's Desire Vocal Gems/with chorus and orchestra, 1935

B8360 As I Sit Here/Sanderson; Love Passes By/Victor Schertzinger, September 1935

B8393 Pale Moon/Logan;The World is Mine Tonight, Posford, George Scott-Wood, OEA2476-7 October 1934

BD405 Romance; Serenata/Friederich Feher/**The Robber Symphony**, January 1936,

B8413 Mifanwy/Forster; At Dawning/Cadman March 1936, OEA2629/30

B8421 Stay with Me Forever/**Giuditta/** Léhar; Vienna, City of My Dreams/Rudolf Sieczynski, Walter Goehr, 21 February 1936, OEA2699/700

B 8435 Ah! Sweet mystery of life/**Naughty Marietta**/Herbert; Say that you are mine/Lockton/Kerrich, May1936

B8442 My Love and I Stand Alone; Sweet Melody of Night/**Give Us This Night**/Korngold, 1936

B8476 I'm all alone/May; I'll wait for you/ Feiner, September 1936

B8498 The way you look tonight/**Swing Time/**Kern; Serenade in the Night/Bixio, November 1936, OEA4067/8

B8520 Land Without Music Vocal Gems, with the Lindonel Three, 1935

B8527 Moon Of Romance/Strachey; A Song For You And Me/Rizzi OEA3951/2, 1937

B8545 A Bird Sang in the Rain/Wood; Undivided
/Thayer, 1937

B8803 Tosca/Strange Harmony of Contrasts; When the
Stars were Brightly Shining/Puccini, Warwick Braithwaite,
LPO, September 1938 OEA1174/5

B8829 Rigoletto/This One or That One; Woman is
Fickle/Verdi,Lawrance Collingwood 1939

B8843 Sadko/Hindu Song/Rimsky Korsakov;
Elegie/Massenet,1938 OEA6982

B8899 One Day When We Were Young/**The Great
Waltz**/Strauss; Sweethearts/**Sweethearts**/Herbert, Clifford
Greenwood, 2 May, 1939, OEA7642

B8920 For You Alone/Geehl; Because/d'Hardelot, Clifford
Greenwood May 1939

B8947 The English Rose/**Merrie England**/German/Clifford
Greenwood; Faery Song/**The Immortal Hour**,Boughton,
John T Cockerill (harp) 18 July 1939

B8968 Macushla/MacMurrough; I'll Walk Beside You/Alan
Murray, Clifford Greenwood, August 1939, OEA8028/9

*B8982 A Paradise For Two/**The Maid of the
Mountains**/Tate; If You Were the Only Girl in the World/ **The
Bing Boys are Here**/Ayer, Clifford Greenwood, 19 October
1939 OEA8119/20,

B8990/BD860 Agnus Dei/Bizet; Ave Maria/Bach-Gounod,
chorus, Herbert Dawson, London PO, Wynn Reeves,
Kingsway Hall, London, November 1939

*B8996 Wanting You/**The New Moon**/Romberg; I'll See You Again/ **Bitter Sweet**/ Coward, Clifford Greenwood, October 1941

B9009 Ay, Ay, Ay/ Freire; Ideale /Tosti, Braithwaite, October 1939

B9022 Bless this House/Brahe; Danny Boy/Weatherly,Herbert Dawson, 1939

B9030 When You Wish Upon a Star/**Pinocchio**/ Harline; Rosita/Kennedy/Carr, 1939

B9031 Indian Summer; A Kiss in the Dark/**The Great Victor Herbert**/Herbert, Ronnie Munro, April 1939, January 1940 OEA8484/5

B9040 Lavender Lass; Love is My Song/Murray, Charles Prentice, May 1940

*B9051 Lover, come back to me/**The New Moon**/Romberg; Ah, Sweet Mystery of Life/ **Naughty Marietta**/ Herbert, Walter Goehr?/Jock Prentice? 7-8 May 1940

B9058 Oh Maiden, My Maiden/**Frederica**/Léhar; Serenade/ **Student Prince**, Romberg, Walter Goehr, November 1939,23 May 1940, OEA8191/2

*B9060 Deep in My Heart, Dear/**The Student Prince** Romberg; Fold your wings/**Glamorous Night**/ Novello, Clifford Greenwood, 8 May 1940

*B9065 Only a rose/**The Vagabond King**/ Friml; You, Just You/**Wild Violets**/Stolz, 7-8 May 1940, OEA 8597/8

B9069 Ah, fill the cup/ Ah, Moon of my delight/ **In a Persian**

Garden, Lehmann,August 1940

*B9070 Love's old sweet song/Molloy; The Second Minuet/Besley, Ronnie Munro, 7-8 May/October 1940, OEA 8610

B9071 Morning; Sylvia/Oley Speaks, Gerald Moore, September 1940

*B9120 Our Greatest Successes Medley 1 The Student Prince/Bitter Sweet, Until/Love's Old Sweet Song/I Hear You Calling Me/Two Little Words OEA8979, 1940

#B9122 Joy of Life/Ivanovici; Tales from the Vienna Woods/Strauss February 1941

B9123 Rose of Tralee/Glover; Phil, the Fluter's Ball/French, Gerald Moore December 1940, OEA 9071/3

B9164 Mountains o' Mourne/French; A Ballynure Ballad/arr Hughes + Trottin' to the Fair/Stanford, Gerald Moore, 1941

B9167 England, Mother England/E C Booth; There's a Land, a Dear Land/Frances Allitsen, Gerald Moore, 1941

B9173 Love, Could I Only Tell Thee/**The Geisha**/Richard Capel; I Hear You Calling Me/Marshall, Gerald Moore, February 1941

*B9177 Love's Garden of Roses/Wood; Will You Remember? **Maytime,** Romberg,Warwick Braithwaite 10 June1941/August 1941

B9193 Passing By/Purcell; Drink to Me Only with Thine Eyes/Trad-Jonson, Gerald Moore, 6 June 1941 OEA9322/3

B9201 When Big Ben Chimes/Kennedy Russell; The Lord's Prayer/Malotte, Gerald Moore, 9 May 1941

*B9202 The Flower; The Golden Song/ **LilacTime/** Schubert/Clutsam, Warwick Braithwaite, 10 June 1941

B9205 Song of Songs/Moya; Trees/Harbach, Gerald Moore, May 1941

*B9226 When we are Married/**The Belle of New York**/Kerker; The Keys of Heaven/Broadwood, September 1941, OEA9533/4

#B9241 Invitation to the Waltz/Weber; Waltz Song/**Tom Jones**/Edward German, *1941*

#B9243 Slumber Song/Schumann/arr Carroll; Song in the Night/Mortimer/Loughborough, Charles Forwood, 1941

B9244 Star of My Soul/**The Geisha**/Jones; To Mary/White, Philip Green, 20 September 1941/June 1942

*B9247 Tristesse: So Deep is the Night/Chopin; My Paradise /**Gangway,** Parr-Davies, Debroy Somers, 20 December 1941, OEA9628

B9255 One Alone/**Desert Song**/Romberg; Song of the Vagabonds/**Vagabond King**/Friml, Debroy Somers, 20 December 1941, OEA9567/8

B9264 Homing/del Riego; Smilin' Through/Penn, Gerald Moore, 1942

B9271 Come Back My Love/Miller/Rubinstein/arr Grün; Will You Go with Me?/Brandon-Park/Murray,Gerald Moore 1942

B9304 Christopher Robin Songs: Down by the Pond, Vespers; Sneezles, Buckingham Palace/Fraser Simpson, with instrumental quintet, 1943

B9315 On Wings of Song/Mendelssohn; Impatience/ Schubert, Gerald Moore, 12 February 1943/1944

*B9326 What is Done/**Lilac Domino**/Cuvillier; Without Your Love/**The Dubarry**/Millocker, Debroy Somers, September 1941 OEA8607

B9342**Four Indian Love Lyrics**/Temple Bells; Less Than the Dust/ Hope-Woodford-Finden/Hubert Greenslade, 1944

B9343 Four Indian Love Lyrics/ Kashmiri Song; Till I Wake Hope-Woodford-Finden/Hubert Greenslade, 1944

*B9370 Barcarolle/ **Tales of Hoffman**/Offenbach; Indian Love Call/**Rose Marie**/Friml, Debroy Somers, 9 March 1944

*B9401Our Greatest Successes 2, 1944

*B9428 Tomorrow; Life begins anew/ **Sweet Yesterday,** Leslie-Smith, Herbert Lodge, 12 July 1945

B9429 Morning Glory, (**Webster Booth**); #Sweet Yesterday, **Sweet Yesterday**, Kenneth Leslie-Smith (**Anne Ziegler**) Adelphi Theatre Orchestra, Herbert Lodge, 12 July 1945

*B9432 Land of Mine; You will return to Vienna/**Waltz Time**/May, 1945

B9451 Eleanore; Unmindful of the roses+Life and Death, ColeridgeTaylor, Hubert Greenslade, 16 November 1945,OEA10750-3

B9458 Just for today/Partridge/Seaver; There is No Death/Johnson/O'Hara, Gerald Moore, 1946

B9472 Bells of St. Mary's/Adams; Parted/Tosti, George Melachrino, 20 March 1946

***B9489** Love Steals Your Heart/ **The Wicked Lady,** May; We'll Gather Lilacs/**Perchance to Dream,** Novello, Jack Byfield 4 June 1946

***B9490** Laugh at Life; Love is the Key/ **The Laughing Lady,** May 1946

B9497 Devotion/Schumann; I Love Thee/Grieg, Gerald Moore, October 1946

B9502 All Soul's Day/ Richard Strauss; Memory Island/ Harrison/ Gerald Moore, September 1946

B9507 Nazareth/Gounod, Herbert Dawson; O, Come All Ye Faithful, Bertram L Harrison, 1946

B9514 Abide With Me; How Lovely are Thy Dwellings/Samuel Liddle, Herbert Dawson, 1946

B9518 Wine song **(Webster Booth); #**I'll Change My Heart **(Anne Ziegler) The Laughing Lady**/May, 1946

B9534 A Perfect Day/Carrie Jacobs-Bond; Always/**Puritan Lullaby**/ Leslie-Smith,May 1947

#B9552 Dearest Love/**Operette**/Coward; O Lovely Night/Ronald, 1947

B9562 O Dry Those Tears/del Riego; Until/Sanderson, 1947

*B9581 Dream Duet/**La Belle Hélène**/ Offenbach; Life and Love/**Princess Charming**/George Posford, April 1947

B9585 Everywhere I Go/ **Four Pastorales**/ Martin, Walter Goehr? Melachrino?;Greensleeves/trad arr Olive Richardson,Eric Robinson 5 November 1946

B9598 Little Road to Bethlehem/Head, Herbert Dawson, orchestra (**Webster Booth**); *Silent Night (**Webster Booth & Anne Ziegler**) 11 June 1947/December 1947

B9617 Nirvana/Adams; My Dreams/Tosti, Eric Robinson 6 August 1947

*B9627 On Wings of Song/Mendelssohn/arr. Doris Arnold; Still as the Night/N/Bohm/arr Doris Arnold, Eric Robinson 22 December 1947, released March 1948

B9633 Break of Day/**Waltz Time**/May; My Heart and I/**Old Chelsea**/Tauber, Jack Byfield February 1946, released April 1948

B9640 Show Me the Way/O'Connor/Morgan; Napoli Bay/Kynoch, George Melachrino, 1948

*B9642 Now is the Hour/Scott; Too Tired to Sleep/Murray, Eric Robinson, 10 March 1948, May 1948

B9703 Wayside Rose/**Frederica**;
Serenade/**Frasquita**/Léhar, December 1948

*B9738 Hear My Song, Violetta/Luckesch/Klose; Love's Last Word is Spoken/Bixio, George Melachrino, 1948

*B9760 Deep in the Heart of a Rose/Horatio Nicholls; The

Fruits of the Earth/Purdell, **National Garden Song**, Geraldo, Eric Robinson, 1949

B9777 If You are There/Ege/North; 'Tis the Day/Leoncavallo Melachrino 1949

*__B9786__ Throw Open Wide Your Window, Dear/Hans May; Song of Paradise/Popplewell/King, Eric Robinson, 1949

*__B9804__ Dearest of All/Vernon Latham Sharp; Music for Romance/**Magyar Melody**/Grün/Maschwitz/Sherwin, Eric Robinson, 1949

*__B9830__ Here in the Quiet Hills/Carne; Take the Sun/**The Glass Mountain**/Rota/, Eric Robinson, 1950

*__B9870__ Swing High, Swing Low; Trot Here and There/ **Véronique**/Méssager, Eric Robinson, 1950

B9999 Drinking Song/**The Rose of Persia**/ Sullivan; Where Haven Lies/**A Princess in Kensington**/German, Mark Lubbbock, 11 July 1950

B10027 I Leave My Heart in an English Garden/**Dear Miss Phoebe**/Harry Parr-Davies**;** I Bless the Day/di Jongh, Mark Lubbock, 20 December 1950,

B10035 May the Good Lord Bless and Keep You/Willson; No More/Yradier/Sidney Torch, 1951

B10092 At the End of the Day; Where'er You Go/O'Keefe, Eric Robinson, 18 May 1951

2/3 HMV C RECORDINGS 12"

C1846 Chappell Ballads/Jack Hylton/ /Herbert Dawson (organ) Webster Booth (with vocal refrain) Side 1 Song of the Bow, Slave Song, **Maire, My Girl** (Webster Booth), Queen of My Heart, Homing, Love's Coronation/Side 2 Intro, Long Ago in Alcala, Where My Caravan Has Rested, **Love's Garden of Roses** (Webster Booth), A May Morning, She is Far From the Land, Chorus Gentlemen, Kingsway Hall, London, 31 January 1930 – 7 February 1930

C2106 Merrie England Vocal Gems/German Side 2 When Cupid First This Old World Trod, **The English Rose,** Webster Booth, **Robin Hood's Wedding,** Webster Booth, **With a Hey, Robin,** Webster Booth, Light Opera Company

C2260 Chu Chin Chow Vocal Gems/Asche/Norton, Light Opera Company, including Stuart Robertson, Webster Booth, 17 March 1931

C2800 Co-optimists Medley/Gideon/Olive Groves, Effie Atherton, Webster Booth, Stuart Robertson, George Scott Wood, 1 October 1935

C2814 Neapolitan Nights, Light Opera Company with Webster Booth

C2827 Memories of Tosti/La Scala Singers with Webster Booth

C2867 This year of Theatreland with Webster Booth, Janet Lind and chorus 2EA4081/2, 1936

C2890 Home and Beauty/Cochrane's Coronation

Review, with Janet Lind, Magda Neeld, Webster Booth. Side 1 **Sing Something in the Morning,** Webster Booth, A Nice Cup of Tea, Twilight Sonata; Side 2 Play it again, **Love me a little today,** Webster Booth, No more, **Sing, Royal Harp,** Webster Booth, 1937

C2903 Theatreland at Coronation Time, with Garda Hall, Stuart Robertson, Sam Costa, Webster Booth. Side 1 Song of the Vagabonds (SR and chorus), Music in May (GH), **At the Balalaika,** Webster Booth, Sing something in the morning (GH and chorus) Side 2 **The Night is Young, and You're so Beautiful,** GH & Webster Booth, I've Got a Thing About You (SC) **If the World were Mine,** Webster Booth, Swing along (SR and chorus), 1937

C2961 Songs That Have Sold a Million, with Foster Richardson, Dorothy Clarke, Webster Booth, December 1937

C3030 La Bohème/Your Tiny Hand is Frozen/Puccini/ **Carmen/**Flower Song/Bizet, Liverpool PO, Warwick Braithwaite, Kingsway Hall, London, 12 September 1938

C3050 Songs That Have Sold a Million (2) with Dorothy Clarke, Foster Richardson, Webster Booth, 1938

C3051 Beneath Her Window Serenade Medley, Walter Goehr/Herbert Dawson. Side 1 Serenade/Drigo, **Serenata/Toselli,** Webster Booth, Serenade/Heykens **Marie, Marie/Di Capua,** Webster Booth; Side 2 Serenade/Schubert, Serenata/ Moszkowski **Serenade in the Night/Bixio,** Webster Booth 1938

C3053 La Bohème/Lovely Maid in the Moonlight/Puccini, with Joan Cross; **Il Trovatore/**Miserere/Verdi, with Joan Cross, Collingwood, Sadlers Wells, Abbey Road, London, 3

November 1938

C3086 Rigoletto/Fairest Daughter of the Graces/Verdi, Quartet with Noel Eadie, Edith Coates, Arnold Matters; **Faust**/Then leave her/Gounod, with Norman Walker, Joan Cross, Collingwood, Sadlers Wells opera chorus and London PO, Studio 1, Abbey Road, London, 3 March 1939

C3087 Messiah/Comfort Ye; Ev'ry Valley/Handel, LPO, Warwick Braithwaite, Kings Hall, London, 28 February/21 March 1939,

C3095 Elijah/Ye People, Rend Your Hearts/If With All Your Hearts; Then Shall the Righteous Shine Forth, Mendelssohn Liverpool PO, Warwick Braithwaite, Kingsway Hall, 28 February, 1939,

C3116 Serenade/Schubert, Ernest Lush; If You Had But Known/Denza, Ernest Lush, Jean Pougnet (violin), 11 August 1939

Ave Maria/Schubert, Ernest Lush (unpublished) - Also recorded on 11 August 1939

C3124 Excelsior, Balfe; Watchman, What of the Night?/Sargeant, with Dennis Noble, male chorus and orchestra, Ronnie Munro, No. 1 Studio, Abbey Road, London, 19 October 1939

C3128 Mikado Vocal Gems, Sullivan, Light Opera Company, with Anne Ziegler, Nancy Evans, Dennis Noble, George Baker; chorus & orchestra, Isadore Godfrey, Kingsway Hall, London, 27 October 1939

C3130 O Friendly Tree/**Serse**, Handel, LPO, Wyn Reeves, 25 July 1939; Lost Chord/Sullivan, Herbert Dawson (organ),

Kingsway Hall, 28 October 1939, December 1939

C3139 Goodbye/Tosti; Liebestraum/Liszt, Warwick Braithwaite, 1940,

C3143 Carmen Vocal Gems/Bizet with Dennis Noble, Noel Eadie, Nancy Evans, Sadlers Wells Orchestra & Chorus conducted by Warwick Braithwaite, Kingsway Hall 21 December 1939

C3151 Gondoliers Vocal Gems/ Sullivan Light Opera Company with Anne Ziegler Nancy Evans, Dennis Noble, George Baker; chorus and orchestra conducted by Isadore Godfrey, Kingsway Hall, London, 27 October 1939

C3171 She is Far From the Land/Lambert, Gerald Moore; Snowy-breasted Pearl/arr Robinson, Charles Prentice,1940

C3196 The Holy City; The Star of Bethlehem/Adams, Bertram Harrison/ Kingsway Hall, London, 6 November 1940/1941

C3261 Take a Pair of Sparkling Eyes/**Gondoliers;** A Wand'ring Minstrel, **Mikado**/Gilbert & Sullivan, Hallé Orchestra, Leslie Heward, Belle Vue, Manchester, 23 September 1941,

C3305 Semele/Where E'r You Walk /Handel; **Saint Paul**/Be Thou Faithful Unto Death/Mendelssohn, Hallé orchestra, Warwick Braithwaite, 28 August 1942, 16 September 1942?

C3309 Faust/All Hail Thy Dwelling, Pure and Holy/Gounod; **Mastersingers**/Prize Song/Wagner Hallé, Braithwaite, 29 August 1942

C3369 La Bohème/ In a Coupé/ Puccini, with Dennis Noble;
Rigoletto/ Caro Nome/Dearest Name/Verdi, Gwen Catley,
Hallé Orchestra, Warwick Braithwaite, Holdsworth Hall,
Manchester 29 August 1942

C3372 Don Giovanni/Mine Be Her Burden; Speak for Me to
My Lady, Mozart, Liverpool PO, Sir Malcolm Sargent, 21
October, 1943,

C3378 Madame Butterfly /Ah, Love Me a Little/Puccini, with
Joan Hammond, Liverpool PO, conducted by Malcolm
Sargent/Liverpool Philharmonic Hall, 21 October 1943

C3379 I Pagliacci/On With the Motley/Leoncavallo, Basil
Cameron, Liverpool PO, 21 December 1943; **Aida/**What If
'Tis I Am Chosen,Heavenly Aida/Verdi Liverpool PO,
Malcolm Sargent, 21 October 1943

C3398 The Barber of Seville/'Tis the Spring of All Invention;
Fifteen My Number Is/Rossini, with Dennis Noble, with
Liverpool PO, Basil Cameron, Philharmonic Hall, Liverpool,
21 December 1943

C3402 Magic Flute/Oh Loveliness Beyond Compare,
Liverpool PO, Sargent, 21 October, 1943; **Il Seraglio/**
Constanze, Constanze/Mozart, Liverpool PO, Philharmonic
Hall, Liverpool, Basil Cameron, 20/21 December 1943,

C3407 Hiawatha's Wedding Feast/ Onaway, Awake
Beloved/ Coleridge-Taylor; **Esmeralda/**O Vision
Entrancing, Goring Thomas, Liverpool PO, Malcolm
Sargent, Philharmonic Hall, Liverpool, 4 July 1944

C3414 Jephtha/Deeper, and Deeper Still; Waft Her, Angels
Through the Skies/Handel, Liverpool PO, Malcolm Sargent,
4 July 1944

C3418 Morgen/R Strauss, Ernest Lush, Alfredo Campoli (violin),11 August 1945; Come into the Garden, Maud/Balfe, Gerald Moore, Studio 3, Abbey Road, London, 9 May 1940 /1945

C3430 Messiah/Thy Rebuke Hath Broken His Heart /Behold and See; He Was Cut Off out of the Land/But Thou Dids't not Leave His Soul in Hell/Handel, City of Birmingham Orchestra, George Weldon, 22 May 1945

*****C3460** Nocturne/Chopin; Liebestraum/ Liszt/arr Besly, Debroy Somers, Studio 1, Abbey Road, London, 15 October, 1945

C3521 Ivor Novello Medley, with Helen Hill, Olive Groves, Peter Graves, Harry Acres, 15 October 1946

C3522 Ivor Novello Medley(2) with Helen Hill, Olive Groves, Peter Graves, Harry Acres, 15 October 1946

C3571 Creation/And God Created Man/In Native Worth Haydn; **Samson**/O Loss of Sight/Total Eclipse/Handel, Stanford Robinson, Kingsway Hall, 7 February 1947

#C3635 Noel Coward Medley with Anne Ziegler, Joyce Grenfell, Graham Payn, Harry Acres, 11 March 1947

#C3636 Noel Coward Medley 2 with Anne Ziegler, Joyce Grenfell, Graham Payn, Harry Acres, 11 March 1947

C3796 Acis and Galatea/Love in Her Eyes Sits Playing, Love Sounds the Alarm/ Handel, Warwick Braithwaite, 8 March 1948,

C3844 God Be in My Head/ Davies;The Long Day Closes, Sullivan,**Tommy Handley Memorial Choir,** February 1949

C3939 Judas Maccabeus/My Arms Against the Gorgios/Sound an Alarm, Braithwaite,18 March 1948; **Samson**/Why Does the God of Israel Sleep? Handel, Stanford Robinson/2 February 1947/December 1949

C3962 Evening song; The Message/Blumenthal, Melachrino 1949

*C4125 Léhar Medley 1: The Merry Widow/Frederica/ The Count Of Luxembourg/ The Land Of Smiles 20 December 1950

2/4 HMV – NUMBERS UNKNOWN

Here Comes the Bride Selection/Schwartz/Light Opera Company with Alice Moxon, Stuart Robertson, Webster Booth, George Baker/Ray Noble/Studio C, Small Queens Hall, London/**Cc18897-4**, 25 March 1930

Irving Berlin Waltz Medley/New Mayfair Orchestra/Ray Noble: Because I love you, **All Alone**, Webster Booth, Always, What'll I do? **The Song is Ended**, Webster Booth, You Forgot to Remember, Studio C, Small Queens Hall, London/ **Bb21098-2/2109922** 22 December 1930

*Love Me Tonight; Tomorrow/**Vagabond King**/Friml, Debroy Somers, 5 January 1943, OEA9587/8

*Blue Smoke/Ruru Karaitiana/ (other side unknown) *I think this was recorded in New Zealand during the 1948 concert tour.*

*The Gates of Paradise; Someday My Heart Will Awake/**King's Rhapsody**/ Novello, Mark Lubbock, 1950

*Lift up Your Hearts/Simpson/Morian; Such Lovely Things/North, Mark Lubbock, 1951

The Night was Made for Love/**The Cat and the Fiddle**/ Kern I cannot trace a number for this – perhaps it is from a broadcast?

***Léhar Medley 2,** Mark Lubbock, 18 January 1951

2/5 LONG PLAYING RECORDS

The Creation/Haydn Monica Hunter, **Webster Booth,** Walter Heinen, St Anne's College (chorus mistress: Mildred Augustyn), Michaelhouse, Pietermaritzburg Philharmonic orchestra (augmented), conducted by Ronald Charles, sleeve notes: Ronald Charles, City Hall, Pietermaritzburg. Recording engineers: A H Hofmeyr, L E De Klerk, Recordings Unlimited, P'maritzburg. 19 September 1964

Elijah/Mendelssohn Monica Hunter, Joyce Scotcher, **Webster Booth,** Wilfred Hutchings, Choral societies of St Anne's (chorus mistress Mildred Augustyn) & Michaelhouse, John Harper (organ), conducted by Barry Smith, sleeve notes: John Morehen, Pietermaritzburg City Hall, 21 September 1963, Gallotone GALP101

The Golden Age of Ballads and Parlour Songs, Miscellaneous singers, including **Webster Booth, Parted,** Tosti, George Melachrino OEA10928-1 B9472 20 March 1946, Sleeve notes: Lyndon Jenkins, EMI1987 GX2554

The Golden Age of Webster Booth, I Bless the Day, Roses of Picardy, Vienna, City of My Dreams, Drink to Me Only, Sweethearts, On Wings of Song, Nirvana, The Faery Song (**The Immortal Hour**), A Perfect Day, Serenade (**The Student Prince**), Passing By, Everywhere I Go, Come into the Garden, Maud, Song of the Vagabonds, Eleanore, I Leave My Heart in an English Garden, At the End of the Day, Sleeve notes: Hugh Palmer, 78s transferred by Peter Brown, EMI GX2547, 1985

Famous British Tenors Miscellaneous singers, including **Webster Booth, O Vision Entrancing (Esmeralda)**, Goring Thomas, Royal Liverpool

PO, Malcolm Sargent, July 1944 Sleeve notes: Grenville Eves, 1970 EMI HQM 1228

Patience/The Gondoliers,
Gilbert and Sullivan, **Gondoliers** (Abridged version) Recorded under the direction of Rupert D'Oyly Carte, Dr Malcolm Sargent. (b) **From the Sunny Spanish Shore**;G Baker, E Ackland, A Moxon, **W Booth, In Enterprise of Martial Kind**-G Baker, A Moxon, N Walker, **W Booth**, b **I Stole the Prince**-S Granville, A Moxon, N. Walker, **W Booth**, G Baker B3867, Sleeve notes: John Freestone, Transferred from 78s by Keith Hardwick, EMI SHB7 4

Irving Berlin Centenary Celebration, **The Great British Dance Bands,** including **Webster Booth, Irving Berlin Waltz medley**, Ray Noble, New Mayfair orchestra, 22 December 1930 EMI 1988 SH512

Webster Booth, The Faery Song, Snowy- breasted Pearl, Temple Bells, O Vision Entrancing, A Bird Sang in the Rain, Take a Pair of Sparkling Eyes, Star of My Soul, When Big Ben Chimes, Onaway! Awake, Beloved, Greensleeves, Come into the Garden, Maud, If You are There, Love is My Song, Where Haven Lies, Always. From collection of Scott Sheldon, 1972, Canada, **Rococo** 5272

Webster Booth: Arias by Handel, Mozart, Verdi, Puccini and Popular Songs
Grove So Beautiful & Stately/Shadows So Sweet (**Serse**), Deeper and Deeper Still/Waft Her, Angels, Through the Skies (**Jephtha**), Where'er You Walk (**Semele**), Mine Be Her Burden, Speak for Me to My Lady (**Don Giovanni**), Ye People, Rend Your Hearts, If With All Your Hearts,(**Elijah**), What If 'Tis I Am Chosen/Heavenly Aida (**Aida**), All Hail, Thou Dwelling, Pure and Lowly (**Faust**), Flower Song (**Carmen**),Your Tiny Hand is Frozen (**La Bohème**), The

Faery Song (**The Immortal Hour**), Take a Pair of Sparkling Eyes (**Gondoliers**), English Rose (**Merrie England**), Onaway! Awake, Beloved (**Hiawatha's wedding feast**), Sleeve notes: John Freestone, compiled from EMI archives by Bryan Crimp,1977, EMI HLM7109 OC O51-06 367M

SWEETHEARTS IN SONG: Anne Ziegler & Webster Booth Only a Rose, Wanting You, Deep in My Heart, Dear, Love Steals Your Heart, Ah! Sweet Mystery of Life, We'll Gather Lilacs, Hear My Song Violetta, Love's Last Word is Spoken, Lover, Come Back to Me, Indian Love Call, I'll See You Again. late fifties, Sleeve notes: Leslie Green   JCLP 10012 EMI (South Africa)

NET MAAR 'N ROOS/Afrikaans
Net Maar 'n Roos/Only a Rose, Laat Ons nie van Liefde Praat/Love's Last Word is Spoken, Al die Soet Geheime/Ah! Sweet Mystery of Life, Diep in My Hart/ Deep in My Heart, Dear, So Donker die Nag/So Deep as the Night, Sal Jy Onthou?/Will You Remember?, Wunderbar, Dit is Verby/One Day When We were Young, Ons Sal Weer Blomme Pluk/We'll Gather Lilacs, Liefling, Kom Terug na My/Lover, Come Back to Me, Die Heildronk van Jou Oë Drink to me only, As die Lente Kom/I'll See You Again, Anne Ziegler, Webster Booth, with Jack Dent (piano) and John Massey (organ), RCA 31,378,Johannesburg, 1960

NURSERY SCHOOL SING-ALONG No. 2
SIDE 1 Songs We Like to Sing, Nursery School Sing Along, I Went to Visit My Friend One Day, We are Busy Washing Linen, This is the Song of the Pirate Ship, Let's Play Cowboys, When We Play at Indians, 3 Down at the Station, The Tugboat, If You Ever See a Whale, The Wheels of the Bus, Aeroplane Song, There are Horses in the Meadow, Tall Buildings in the Town, The Miner, SIDE 2 Zoom, Zoom, Yodel-Elli-Oh, Frère Jacques, 2 On the Bridge of Avignon,

Chinese Music, In China People Plant Rice, Bread is a Lovely Thing to Eat, Will You be a Sailor Man? If I Could Have a Windmill, Dutch Wooden Shoes, I Had a Little Engine, Our Percussion Band, Nursery School Sing Along. Anne Ziegler and Webster Booth, assisted by Michael Murray, Peter Robinson and the Nazareth House Children's Chorus, conducted by Sylvia Sullivan, Heinz Alexander (piano). Presentation arranged by Gwen Murray, 1963 Gallo EKL20

MUSIC FOR ROMANCE – ANNE ZIEGLER & WEBSTER BOOTH The Flower, The Golden Song (**Lilac Time, Schubert**), Love Me Tonight, Tomorrow (**The Vagabond King-Friml**) What is Done You Never Can Undo (**Lilac Domino-Cuvillier**), Without Your Love (**Dubarry-Millocker**) Dearest Love (**Operette-Coward**) Liebestraum (**Dream of Love- Liszt, arr Besley**), Nocturne, (**Chopin, arr Besley**), Music for Romance (**Magyar Melody-Sherwin**), Lehar Medley, Life and Love (**Princess Charming-Sirmay**), Dream Duet (**La Belle Helene-Offenbach**), Throw Open Wide Your Window, Dear, (May) produced, compiled and transferred by Chris Ellis, Cover notes: Ralph Harvey, Encore, EMI records, 1980, ONCM 530 OC(054-07-228)

SWEETHEARTS IN SONG: ANNE ZIEGLER & WEBSTER BOOTH If You Were the Only Girl in the World, A Paradise for Two, Wanting You, I'll See You Again, Lover, Come Back To Me, Ah! Sweet Mystery of Life, Fold Your Wings, Deep in My Heart, Dear, Only a Rose, You, Just You, Love's Old Sweet Song, Will You Remember, When We are Married, So Deep is the Night, Barcarolle, Indian Love Call, Love Steals Your Heart, We'll Gather Lilacs, Hear My Song, Violetta, produced, compiled and transferred by Chris Ellis, Sleeve notes: Peter Gammond 1979 **Encore, EMI records 1979** ONCM519 OC-054-06 936M

2/6 COMPACT DISCS

The following CDs were issued from the late 1980s when the original 78s were over fifty years old and going out of copyright. If you put in a search for these CDs on the Internet you should be able to obtain a new or second hand copy.

WEBSTER BOOTH & ANNE ZIEGLER ON CD

WEBSTER BOOTH – MOONLIGHT AND YOU, Flapper, Past CD9709 (issued in 1989)
WEBSTER BOOTH in Opera and Song, Memoir Classics CDMOIR435
WEBSTER BOOTH HANDEL ARIAS, OPERATIC ARIAS Dutton CDLX7032
JOAN CROSS & WEBSTER BOOTH Loveliness beyond compare, The Greenhorn Record Company 0008
DRAWING ROOM BALLADS, Track 2: A brown bird singing, Wood, Track 6: Smilin' through, Penn, 15: At Dawning, Cadman, Track 20: Song of songs, Moya, Track 24: Goodbye, Tosti, *Webster Booth*
THREE GREAT TENORS Josef Locke, Richard Tauber, Webster Booth, EMI 7243 8 34676 2 4

There are also a number of compilation CDs which feature Webster Booth in one or two tracks. These are:

ROYAL LIVERPOOL PHILHARMONIC (1840-1990) Track 6: Onaway! Awake, beloved (Hiawatha's Wedding Feast) Coleridge-Taylor, Webster Booth EMI CDM763370 2 (issued 1990)
A TRIBUTE TO DENNIS NOBLE Track 5: 'Tis the Spring (Barber of Seville) Rossini, with Webster Booth. Dutton CDLX 7017

A PORTRAIT OF NORMAN WALKER Track 10: Then Leave Her (Faust) Gounod, with Joan Cross and Webster Booth Dutton CDLX 7021

STARS OF ENGLISH OPERA in the 1930s and 40s Track 10: O Vision Entrancing (Esmerelda) Goring Thomas, *Webster Booth* Dutton CDLX 7018

STARS OF ENGLISH OPERA Volume Two Track 16: Misere (Il Trovatore) Verdi, with Webster Booth and Joan Cross, Track 17: Quartet (Rigoletto) Verdi, with Noel Eadie, Edith Coates, Webster Booth and Arnold Matters Dutton CDLX 7020

STARS OF ENGLISH ORATORIO Track 10: And God Created Man/In Native Worth (The Creation) with Webster Booth Dutton CDLX 7025

MALCOLM SARGENT conducts Mendelssohn's ELIJAH CD 2 Track 19: Ye people, Rend Your Hearts; If With All Your Hearts, Track 23: Then Shall the Righteous Shine Forth, Webster Booth

DEBROY SOMERS AND HIS BAND Night Time Brings Dreams of You, Track 19: West End Nights – Vocal Gems: Gay Deceivers (medley); You are Me Serenade; Stop Press (medley): You and the Night and the Music, Easter Parade, with Webster Booth, Muriel Barron, Marjorie Stedeford, chorus, Living Era CD AJA 5616 (issued in 2006)

CDs BY ANNE ZIEGLER AND WEBSTER BOOTH

ANNE ZIEGLER & WEBSTER BOOTH Love's Old Sweet Song, Flapper Past CD7034

ANNE ZIEGLER & WEBSTER BOOTH Deep In My Heart, Music & Memories MMD 1044 (issued 1996)

ANN (sic) ZIEGLER & WEBSTER BOOTH Love's Old Sweet Song EMI 7243 8 28434 2 9 (issued 1995)

ANNE ZIEGLER & WEBSTER BOOTH EMI100 7243 8 56897 2 7 (issued 1997)

WEBSTER BOOTH & ANNE ZIEGLER Along the Road to Dreams Living Era CD AJA 5365 (issued 2001)

2/7 BROADCASTS AVAILABLE ON TAPE OR RECORD in NATIONAL SOUND ARCHIVE OR PRIVATE COLLECTIONS

1936
Voice of Romance/ Fred Hartley's quintet, Webster Booth, Anne Ziegler presented by James Dyrenforth, radio broadcast (circa 1936) (Private collection)

1938
Hugh the Drover/Vaughan Williams/Rose Alper, WB, Excerpts from Act 2, 1 November 1938 (National Sound Archive)

1940s
#Down in the Forest/Landon Ronald/Music Hall, 8 June 1946 BBC
Earl and the Girl, The/Queen of June/Ivan Caryll,Music Hall broadcast
*Floradora/Dolores/Leslie Stuart, Music Hall broadcast
*Gypsy Love/Léhar/ Music Hall Radio broadcast
#Invitation to the Waltz/Weber (Live, with Charles Forwood at the piano)
*Merry Widow Waltz/Léhar BBC Music Hall broadcast
#Pink Lady Waltz/Caryll/Radio Music Hall broadcast
#Stormy Weather/Harold Arlen and Ted Koehler, Music Hall, BBC broadcast
Two eyes of blue/ Music Hall broadcast
You are my heart's delight/Land of Smiles/Léhar/ Music Hall broadcast (Private collection)

1951
*Festival of variety 6 May 1951 (National Sound Archive)

1952
Music Hall with Derek Roy, Percy Edwards, Anne Ziegler, Webster Booth, Sid Millward and his Nitwits, Jean Kennedy. *The Big Top, The pawn shop on the corner.* **31 May 1953, BBC Broadcast (2 sided disc) 78rpm** (National Sound Archive)

1962
*Ah, Leave Me not to Pine/Gilbert & Sullivan/ Lord Oom Piet, film soundtrack – interrupted)
The Battle Eve/Theo Bonheur/Graham Burns,WB/Anna Bender/ Drawing Room SABC April 1962
*Drink to Me Only, Anna Bender/Drawing Room/SABC April 1962
Friend o' Mine/Sanderson/WB/Anna Bender/ Drawing Room SABC April 1962
#He'll Say That for My Love/Xerses/Handel, Anna Bender/Drawing Room/SABC April 1962
#Little Damozel/Novello/ Anna Bender/Drawing Room Broadcast SABC
If You had but Known/Denza/Anna Bender/Walter Mony (violin) Drawing Room SABC April 1962
Kashmiri Song/Woodford-Finden/ Anna Bender/
Drawing Room SABC April 1962
My Dreams/Tosti/ Anna Bender/ Drawing Room SABC April 1962
O Dry Those Tears/del Riego/ Anna Bender/Drawing Room SABC April 1962
*The Second Minuet/Besly, Anna Bender/Drawing Room/SABC April 1962
The Sweetest Flower that Blows/Peterson/Hawley/ Anna Bender/ Drawing Room SABC April 1962
Watchman, What of the Night?/Sarjeant/ Graham Burns, Drawing Room SABC April 1962 (Private collection)

1966
*Bitter Sweet selection/Coward Johannesburg City Hall, SABC orchestra conducted by Edgar Cree
#Drink to me only/SABC orchestra conducted by Edgar Cree, City Hall Johannesburg SABC
Holy City/Adams/SABC orchestra conducted by Edgar Cree, City Hall/Johannesburg/SABC (Private collection)

1968
Elijah/Excerpts/Mendelssohn, Knysna Choral Society, Dudley Holmes, Ena van der Vyver, Webster Booth (singing baritone). Private recording at concert, Knysna.
Messiah/Excerpts/Handel, Knysna Choral Society, Recits: Anne Ziegler, Thy Rebuke Hath Broken His Heart/Behold and See, **Webster Booth**, piano
accompaniment, private recording at concert. Knysna.

Merrie England/It is the Merry Month of May/ German, Ena van der Vyver, **Webster Booth,**
Tales of Hoffman/Barcarolle/Offenbach, Ena van der Vyver, **Anne Ziegler,** Private recording at Knysna concert, late 1960s.

1979
*I Remember it Well/Gigi/ Lerner & Loewe, various BBC broadcasts, late 1970s.
*Merry Widow Waltz/ Léhar BBC broadcasts, late 1970s
Mifanwy/Forster BBC broadcast
*My Dearest Dear/Novello BBC broadcasts, late 1970s
#The Poplar/Mark Lubbock, BBC broadcast
*We'll Gather Lilacs/Perchance to Dream/Novello BBC broadcasts, late 1970s (Private collection)

1983
TV Broadcast **title:ONLY A ROSE**
Booth, Webster, 1902-1984 (speaker, male; interviewee)

Ziegler, Anne (speaker, female; interviewee)
Hogg, James (speaker, male; interviewer)
Soundtrack to the television interview, Webster Booth's last television appearance, in which he and his wife talk about their career together with James Hogg.
BBC television recording (sound only) broadcast BBC2 July 31 1984. (National Sound Archive)

Anne Ziegler & Webster Booth (1978)